Can't Live Without

by

JOANNE PHILLIPS

Wonderful Books

Wonderful Books
ISBN 9798570128477

KDP Paperback Edition 2020

This book is dedicated to all readers of romantic fiction - you keep the dream alive and give me a reason to keep writing!

To find out more about this series, check out my Author Note *at the back of the book.*

Chapter 1

Stella

Ever heard the saying, 'If you can't stand the heat get out of the kitchen'? What would you do if this wasn't just a philosophical suggestion but a blazing fact staring you in the face one morning as you wander downstairs to make yourself a cup of tea?

Shall I tell you how I react when I nudge open my kitchen door and see yellow flames climbing up my kitchen units? I'm a thirty-seven-year-old single mother, responsible and capable and – I thought until now – calm in the face of most crises. So I stand in the doorway for a second or two, gape-mouthed and wide-eyed, allowing the heat to sear my shocked retinas. I drop last night's half-empty coffee cup from my slack hand and watch it shatter on the slate floor. Then, without a single coherent thought, I race back through the house, out of the front door and into the street, screaming like a schoolgirl.

I immediately forget everything I've ever learned about fire safety.

There is, I'm pretty sure, a small and shiny red extinguisher languishing under the sink. There are procedures for this sort of thing: wet blankets to be thrown, doors to be closed, valuables to be lifted and removed (although even if I'd had the presence of mind it would probably have been a struggle to get my American double-door ice-maker fridge-freezer out in time).

Never mind that I'm not even dressed, or that the nightshirt I'm wearing isn't my own but my seventeen-year-old daughter's and therefore about three sizes too small. Never mind that I haven't yet brushed my hair or cleaned my teeth. You don't worry about these things when your house is on fire.

I run directly into the arms of my neighbour, the ridiculously handsome but slightly obsessive man from Number Four. Gasping and reaching back to point over my shoulder I manage the words, 'Fire!' and 'Help!'

He looks beyond me to see smoke streaming out of my kitchen window and then drops me like a hot brick and runs back into his own house, hopefully to call the fire brigade.

More people dribble out to see what's going on. The handsome neighbour joins us again, a mobile phone pressed to his ear, giving my address in a clear, calm voice I find deeply impressive.

'I'm so sorry,' he says to me. Like someone's died.

I don't know his name, only that he's lived next door to me in Chaplin Grove for six months and that he cleans his car (sporty, red, expensive) at least twice a week and shops only at Waitrose. We stand side by side and watch the smoke billow out of my front door, thickening to a grey-white fog.

'Your daughter...?' He is still staring at my house.

'She's away,' I answer shakily. Did the man think I'd be standing here relatively calmly while my daughter burnt to death inside? 'She's at her father's,' I explain unnecessarily.

The sight of actual flames creeping around the side wall finally spurs me into action. The sense of unreality slips away as I realise what is happening. My house is being destroyed.

'Shit!' I cry.

Suddenly I know I must get back inside the house and salvage ... something. This is more than just a minor incident, a little blip that can be sorted out with a good clean and a lick of paint. All my worldly possessions are inside those brick walls, not to mention all Lipsy's worldly possessions: her

2

Playstation, her DVD player, her iPod, her computer...

My daughter is going to kill me.

Mr Waitrose pulls me back before I reach the door. The flames have got there first anyway. An orange haze glimmers in the hall, coming off the walls like phosphorous. In a completely deranged way it's quite beautiful.

I hear sirens in the distance and my heart lifts just a little. Maybe the damage won't be too bad after all. Maybe they'll catch it in the nick of time. I look around at my neighbours for reassurance, my face a hopeful question mark. They each wear an identical expression of horror and, like the psychic I'm most definitely not, I can read their one single thought: Thank goodness it isn't my house.

***

When fire engines start to pile up, I am ushered across the road by a lady with white lacquered hair. She installs me on her sofa, sits next to me and strokes my hand, making noises I think are supposed to calm me down. 'There, there, dear,' she says every few seconds. Sitting stiffly upright I stare straight ahead, eyes unfocused, ears ringing with the sound of sirens. Her voice is far away. She doesn't manage to calm me down.

We're in her house, the grand one on the corner. I've seen her taking her miniature poodle out for walks. They look similar, in the way dogs and their owners sometimes do. A small group of self-appointed protectors, of whom Mr Waitrose seems to be the leader, has followed us here. We all smell of smoke, like the aftermath of burnt toast and a greasy roast dinner. Only worse.

Much, much worse.

I rub my stinging eyes with tight fists and look around the room. The four other residents of Chaplin Grove are here: newly married couple Pete and Louise, their faces pinched and anxious; a middle-aged woman who has lived at Number One for only a month; and Mr Waitrose of course. I'm Stella

3

Hill and I live at Number Three. The house with three enormous water hoses currently aimed at its roof.

Poodle Lady seems quite animated, making the most of her role as unofficial trauma counsellor by going over who'd seen what and when. She says, 'I was putting out the washing when I said to Bill, "I can smell smoke", and he said to me, "You're imagining it, woman, your sense of smell is as bad as that bloody dog's." Well, you can imagine how he feels now. If he'd listened to me ...'

I watch her as if from a long way away. I want to go back to my house, watch over it, survey the damage for myself, see if anything can be salvaged. Thoughts of all that we might have lost are crowding my mind now and making it difficult to think clearly. I feel I'm going to collapse under the weight of it all.

I try to get up but Mr Waitrose won't let me. He tells me to stay where I am and the others agree with him. Their words fly around me like panicky birds as they exchange wild ideas about how the fire might have started. Have they forgotten I'm even here? They'll probably still be talking about it weeks from now, an exciting morning, a break from the old routine. Of course they are glad it didn't happen to them, but do they have to be so *vocally* glad?

Resentment stirs ugly inside me. Maybe they sense it; the atmosphere changes slightly and they shift their collective attention back to me.

'At least you're OK, though. You weren't hurt.' This comes from the anonymous lady, our newest resident. She has kind eyes and wears long, hippy-style skirts. True enough, I think, although I'll reserve judgement on the psychological damage.

'Thank goodness it didn't happen in the middle of the night while you were asleep!' says Louise in her mouse-like voice, clutching her husband's hand so tightly she looks likely to break it off.

I nod to show her I agree that, yes, not being burned to

4

death in your sleep is indeed a good thing.

'Oh well, it could have been worse,' says Poodle Lady. She says it kindly, absently, but something about the way it just slips off her tongue enrages me and I suddenly find my voice.

'You think?' I snap, twisting round to stare at her. 'It could have been better, though. For me, at least. For example, it could have been *your* house instead.'

Unforgivable, I know.

My outburst is met with a stunned silence, but perversely I am glad to have shut them all up. Little pinpricks of anger make me almost enjoy lashing out. It releases some of the tension. Not much, but now I feel slightly less trapped. And my resolve is returning.

It's short-lived.

Something else I've observed before is how resilient people can be when they feel sorry for you. My rescuers rally with cries of how I have every right to be upset, and I should let it all out, that's OK. I give up and slump back into the over-stuffed sofa. I feel weightless, unreal. Maybe this is all a dream. Maybe I'll wake up in a minute in my bed, my super-soft duvet wrapped around me like a cloud, fuzzy and contented, the whole weekend stretching out ahead of me ...

I notice a Swiss-style cuckoo clock on the wall above the Poodle Lady's TV. It has tiny, intricately carved wooden doors painted green, and red decoupage flowers on the roof. It is hideous. I imagine the little wooden bird popping out on the hour and crying, 'Help me, help me!' instead of cuckoo. It's 9.55 am.

I sit up, determination making my movements careful and deliberate. This is not a dream – and I am not going to be cuckooed at while my house burns to the ground. I'm ready to face the music, and more than ready to fend off any further objections. I perch myself on the edge of the sofa and grip the cushion edges with shaky hands.

'Right,' I say. And then, more loudly, 'Excuse me?' But then I glance down and remember that I'm still wearing

Lipsy's nightshirt – the pink one with "I Am A Sex Goddess" emblazoned across the front in gold lettering – and I see that I have brown stains across my lap from the chocolate I indulged in last night, making the most of a rare moment of peace and quiet. On my feet are my favourite, almost threadbare, pink fluffy slippers: a Christmas present from years back when my daughter still believed in giving *and* receiving.

Looking up I find Mr Waitrose's eyes also trained on the slippers, an amused smile hovering around his clearly defined mouth.

Just perfect.

There may have been times when I've felt lower than I do right now but I can't remember when. With everything I own gone up in smoke – my dignity along with it – I have descended to a whole new level of having a crap life. But the great thing about reaching the bottom is: there's only one way to go.

* * *

'So, everything is gone? Everything?'

Monday morning and I am sitting in the staffroom holding court for my horrified colleagues at Smart Homes. Susan, the most recent addition to our happy group, is having trouble taking it all in.

'Yep,' I say. 'Absolutely everything.'

Although strictly speaking I suppose this isn't true. Some of my possessions still exist – not everything burnt to ashes in the fire. But what remains is completely useless. One of the firemen, still smeared with soot and smelling of damp dog, told me that if the fire and the smoke hadn't got them, the water damage would have seen them off.

'Even your shoes?' says Susan, almost unable to bear the enormity of this.

'Even my shoes. Except for these, of course.'

I am wearing a pristine pair of Reeboks, which thankfully escaped the fire by residing in the boot of my car in a rarely used gym bag. I'm also wearing the cycling shorts and vest-top from said gym bag, as these are currently the only wearable clothes I possess. It must be pretty obvious to everyone that they've been in the boot of my car for some time, not only because of the slightly musty smell but also because they clearly fitted me a lot better when I was actually bothering to go to the gym regularly.

I swing around in the swivel chair and lift my legs onto the table to show off the trainers. Joe's eyes nearly pop out of his head.

'Oh, put it away, Stella.'

This is Loretta, the office bitch. She always acts this way when someone else is the centre of attention. I leave my legs where they are. Last season's workout gear probably isn't ideally suited to the office but I can't let the comment go.

'I'm sorry that I can't stick to the office *dress code* today, Loretta. I'm afraid all of my clothes were completely ruined in the *fire*.'

The others murmur sympathetically and Susan pats me on the arm. I tilt my head up towards Loretta and raise an eyebrow provocatively.

She gives me a look that implies she thinks my usual attire isn't that much better than today anyway and, putting on the vocal equivalent of six sugars, asks, 'Was that what you were wearing when it happened? You don't look like you've seen the inside of a gym for quite some time.'

The staffroom becomes very quiet. Loretta and I have locked horns before and it is never pretty. But I don't have the energy for it today and she knows it. She stands over me, hands on bony hips, a smirk planted on a face that definitely lost the fight with the ugly stick.

I swing my legs off the table quickly, making her jump out of the way, and I stand up, a good three inches taller than her.

'Yes, Loretta. I was wearing this on Saturday morning.'

Thank God she wasn't there to see me in Lipsy's nightshirt and my fluffy slippers. 'And I'll probably be wearing it quite a lot from now on, it being the only outfit I've got left. If you don't like it I suggest you take it up with Paul.'

We eyeball each other for a few long seconds, your classic Mexican stand-off. She opens her mouth to speak, no doubt something devastatingly clever and cutting on the tip of her tongue. I am saved by a cheerful voice from the doorway.

'Hey, Stella. Love the new look!'

Paul Smart. Owner of Smart Homes, my boss of eleven years, and one of my best friends for even longer. He acts like he's just walked in but I'm sure he's heard everything and timed it just right. He makes a habit of getting me out of tight spots: he's done it so many times he occupies the number one position on my speed-dial.

Loretta closes her mouth tightly and her lips all but disappear.

'You've given me an idea, Stella,' Paul says in his usual upbeat way. 'Every Monday we could all wear our gym stuff to work and go for a communal jog at lunchtime. It would liven us up at bit, don't you think?'

The atmosphere lightens a few kilograms and I smile triumphantly as Loretta stomps away. A battle won or an enemy made? Only time will tell. It occurs to me that even with much bigger, more important things to worry about I can still get drawn into the petty stuff. In a way, it's kind of reassuring.

As the staffroom empties Paul takes me to one side.

'Tea?' His blue eyes are warm and full of sympathy. I nod gratefully. 'So, are you planning on going jogging later?'

I flop back into the chair and sigh. 'I'm sorry, Paul. I know it looks crappy to come into work like this. It was either these or nothing, I'm afraid. Why is everyone I know so much smaller than me?'

None of my mother's clothes were suitable to borrow – not that I'd really want to don her frilly blouses and bias-cut skirts – and my best friend, Bonnie, only comes up to my armpit. Lipsy enjoyed raiding Bonnie's designer-stocked wardrobe though, which distracted her from berating me for all of half an hour.

'"Nothing" would have been OK by me,' says my boss with a cheeky grin.

Paul's an outdoorsy kind of man, you know the type: runs every morning, plays football in the park on a Sunday with his mates, sports a natural tan and sun-kissed hair even in the middle of winter.

If I was a man I'd hate him. But I'm just a lowly employee, so I throw a Bourbon at him instead.

'Hey, don't waste them.' He puts it back in the biscuit tin and closes the lid. 'You're going to need these, Stella, to get you through today.'

How well he knows me. I watch as Paul makes tea: skimmed milk and two sugars for me, which always makes him smile.

'So, you're back at your mother's?' he says, handing me my mug and grimacing.

I nod, squirming inside at how that sentence makes it seem as though I only left my parents' house a few weeks ago. On the contrary, Lipsy and I have been living in our own home for thirteen years. One small set-back like a house fire and you're back in the room you grew up in, asking if there's enough hot water for a bath and watching TV programmes you can't stand in a lounge filled with enough memories to suffocate you.

I'm not ungrateful. I'm lucky to have a roof over my head. It just makes me feel as though the last thirteen years never happened: all those steps forward, all those hard-fought battles. What was the point when one small step takes you all the way back to where you started from, like a life-size game of snakes and ladders?

And with a furious seventeen-year-old daughter to contend with the last thing I need is to feel like a child again

9

myself.

Paul will understand. He knows all about going it alone. He built this business from scratch with nothing more than a love of property and a business enterprise loan to guide him. I open my mouth, ready to share my innermost thoughts. Unfortunately, Joe chooses that precise moment to walk back into the staffroom, humming under his breath.

'The worst thing is, though,' I say loudly, 'I have absolutely no underwear left now.'

Joe freezes, turns tomato red and races for the door. Mission accomplished.

Paul raises an eyebrow. 'Lipsy not taking it well, then?' As predicted, he hits the nail on the head with painful accuracy.

'She hates me. I mean, she wasn't too keen on me before but I just put that down to teenage rebellion. All kids hate their parents, right? At least, they hate the one they're with – the absent one gets off scot-free.' With an effort, I bring myself back to the matter in hand. 'You should have seen her face, Paul. I had to watch as she went through in her head every single thing she'd lost, and there was nothing I could do about it.'

'It's only stuff, Stella. Stuff can be replaced.'

'She's a child. She believes stuff is all she has. It's what gives her kudos with her friends. You know what she's like, what all kids are like these days. She looked at me as though I'd gone into her room and personally set the fire myself.'

Of all the images that would haunt me from the weekend, the reproach in Lipsy's eyes was the worst. It was as if she knew before I even summoned up the courage to tell her, how much worse it was about to get.

Paul takes my hand and fills it with biscuit. 'It wasn't your fault, Stella. These things happen. When the insurance pays out, you and Lipsy can go on a huge shopping spree. Think of the fun you'll have, spending all that money, getting everything new. You're just as bad as her, you know, Mrs Must-Have-The-Very-Best-Of-Everything. Come on, admit it

– if you'd had the chance you'd have chosen to save your new sofa over the family photos.'

He is teasing me but I can't meet his eyes. Close, Mister, but no cigar. I'm picturing my beloved fridge-freezer, ruined forever along with everything else I'd worked so hard for. Funnily enough, the photos were one of the few things to survive, just a little bit of water damage curling up the edges.

Why do I find it so hard to derive any comfort from this? I'm disgusted with myself, but I just can't help it. I struggled so hard, for so long, to buy comfort for Lipsy and me, to buy the right things, the things that other, normal, families have, and I can't get my head around the fact that it is all gone. And all I have left is exactly what I had before. It's like someone has reached inside me and pulled out a decade of my life. I'm empty, and a few soggy photos are not going to make me feel better.

Plus, Paul's blithe assertion that Lipsy and I can simply go shopping again to make ourselves feel better is way off the mark. If only that were the case.

I take a deep breath, and in my smallest voice, I tell Paul what I've done. Or rather, what I haven't done. He frowns, leans forward, says, 'Pardon?'

I tell him again. There is no hiding from this one.

'I – erm – I didn't actually have any insurance.'

And there it is: my unforgivable crime. This is no ordinary calamity, to be fixed with a couple of phone calls and a few months' discomfort. Oh no, when I say all our possessions are gone forever, I mean.

Paul says, 'Are you insane?'

Quite possibly.

But try not to judge me too harshly. There are worse things a person can do than let their house insurance lapse. If you knew what I'd been through the last few years you might be a little more understanding.

Chapter 2

Lipsy

Taking the small, ring-bound notebook out of its paper bag, Lipsy stroked its smooth black cover thoughtfully. As her new diary it would do fine, but nothing in this world could replace her old fake-leather one with the press stud flap. Or the one before that – candy stripes with teddy bears waving from the corner of each page. Lipsy had filled more than ten diaries, starting them practically as soon as she could write. She couldn't believe they were gone forever. Just couldn't believe it.

If she closed her eyes she could picture the diaries as they were only a week ago, stacked high up on her bookcase, away from prying eyes. She trusted her mum not to look at them.

Now it seemed that might have been the only thing she could trust her with.

The girl moved around the bedroom, picking up and replacing random objects: a pink teddy pyjama holder, its tummy deflated and hollow-looking; a tiny straw basket filled with dusty china flowers; a paper cowgirl hat hanging on the back of the door, bent and flattened out of shape. At least this room was full of familiar things, which helped a little. Here, in her grandma's house, she felt comfortable and safe and – most importantly – left alone.

But all these things belonged to a younger Lipsy: an unhappy, unpopular girl whose family was falling apart. This

13

past year, Lipsy had managed to mould herself into someone who fitted in – who was admired, envied even, by her friends. She had left her childhood behind. Cowgirl hats and teddies were for children. Lipsy was a woman.

The *new* Lipsy always wore the right clothes, always knew the latest slang, the best put-downs, the newest swear words. She listened to the coolest bands, made sure she knew enough about what mattered to impress other people but never enough to sound nerdy. She'd successfully left behind the burden of her fractured family and she damn well wasn't going to let this bloody fire set her back again.

The pages of the new diary were cool and smooth. Lipsy loved a brand-new notebook, untouched and waiting. She tapped the pen between her teeth and thought of how to begin. This diary would very probably be published one day when she was rich and famous and people wanted to read the fascinating story of how she got to where she was from being a one-parent child with a no-good father, a crazy mother, a jailbird granddad, a spendaholic grandma, and an uncle who was only one step up from a tramp.

If these details were exaggerated a bit, well, that was OK. It was her story, after all. And the chapter where their house burnt to the ground, and Lipsy and her poor, slightly mental, faded-beauty of a mother lost every single thing they owned, would have the public riveted, she just knew it.

Lipsy sighed, running a finger under each eye to check that her make-up wasn't smudged. She was trying hard to turn this into something positive, she really was. Her grandma's lodger, Alistair, had told her that the grown-up way to deal with disaster was to turn it into a positive. She liked the sound of the word "disaster" and decided to make it the title of this first chapter in her new diary.

But it was harder than she'd expected. Her thoughts kept returning to the sight of her bedroom two days ago. Dirty water streaking down the walls where she'd carefully pasted her posters and her collection of art cards. The shelf of pulpy, unreadable diaries. Her computer was ruined, they told her, although it looked OK, just a bit wet. Well, of course it couldn't survive that drenching.

'But the bloody fire didn't even reach up here,' she had screamed at her mum, who stood in the doorway still wearing one of Lipsy's cast-off nighties. Looking ridiculous, as usual. 'Why did they have to destroy everything in *my* room?'

'My room's ruined too, sweetie,' came the reply. In what way did that make it any better? Her mum's bedroom had been just that – a room with a bed in it and some clothes. And all her mum's stuff was rubbish anyway: those stupid trouser suits she liked to wear, the tops that *mimicked* fashion but never got it quite right. Lipsy's room contained all her worldly belongings and it was plain to see that the firemen had no right to go flinging water about willy-nilly like that.

Not that she blamed them, oh no. The blame for the fire – the *devastating* fire – lay firmly at the feet of one person. Her mother. She may not have set it herself deliberately, but Lipsy did not doubt that it would turn out to have been caused by some failing on her part. As for the other thing, Lipsy understood enough about insurance to know that not having any was just about the worst thing a person could do. It meant that whereas a normal family would simply go out and start again with new things, Lipsy couldn't. And that was unforgivable.

She placed the pen carefully against the clean white surface of the paper and began to write:

Monday 4th June 4.30 pm

Lipsy Hill's Diary – How I Survived Disaster

She wrote with her head bent low to the child's desk, her sleek dark hair falling across her face as she mouthed the words silently, unconsciously. When she'd finished three pages she sat back, stretching her narrow body like a dancer. And then, furiously, she began writing again, this time a list, in no particular order, with the heading:

Things I Can't Possibly Live Without …

***

Stella

At lunchtime I go shopping. Strangely enough, I don't enjoy this experience, probably because I'm spending money I don't have on things that give me absolutely no pleasure to buy. Functional knickers and bras, a pair of jeans and a pair of wear-everywhere shoes. A few plain T-shirts. Some socks. Boring! This is a capsule-sized capsule wardrobe. In Monsoon I splash out on a chiffon blouse in cheerful citrus colours. I just need something to brighten up my day.

There's no point buying anything for Lipsy. She thinks I have less than no taste and would no doubt roll her eyes disgustedly at any offering I might make. Besides, she is OK in the clothes department for the moment. When I dragged her round to Bonnie's yesterday she spent a peaceful hour going through my best friend's wardrobe, oohing and ahhing over her collection of designer clothes, shoes and handbags. Pocket-sized Bonnie and Lipsy are roughly the same size, and Bonnie, generous as ever, allowed my daughter to put together her own capsule wardrobe, drawing the line only at a designer handbag, as worn by Mischa Barton. I tried on one or two items myself but ended up looking as though I'd just been through the hot-wash cycle, much to Lipsy's disgust.

I guess I'm going to have to get used to Lipsy's disgust.

Paul has given me an advance on my wages, something he's been doing a lot lately, and I can't see how I'm going to stop needing this gesture anytime soon. I've known Paul Smart since I was fourteen; we went to the same high school. He was a real heart-throb back then, you know the sort: leather jacket even when it's thirty degrees outside, girls standing in clusters giving him sly smiles, other boys trying to impress him by picking on the skinny girl with the buck teeth from two years below. Who, believe it or not, was me. I know, you've got a picture in your head that I'm drop-dead gorgeous. Well, I am. (Modesty requires me to say that I'm joking.) But back then, in the dark days, I had legs like sticks and teeth that wouldn't look out of place on Bugs Bunny. Thank goodness for wealthy parents and good dentistry.

Paul never participated in the bullying. He was my hero, uber-cool, always made a point of saying hello to me, causing my little group of misfit friends to swoon. For a while, I thought I was in love with him – until I was eighteen, in fact. He treated me like the younger sister he didn't have. My love was unrequited, and that hurt.

One weekend, during the only year I managed to complete at university, I was visiting home and I saw him around town. I was in a bar with a group of crazy friends, showing off and being annoying, you know how you do. One of the girls started making faces at some guys sitting at a table nearby, and then she was laughing and calling them boring old farts. Apparently, they'd been giving us the evil eye for being too loud. I looked over with my who-do-you-think-you-are killer stare and realised one of them was Paul.

I was gobsmacked. I mean, he was so normal. And I realised there and then that he was just a guy. Special, but nobody special. Which was how he'd always thought of me, I guess.

We stayed in touch after that, and when I'd had Lipsy, and loved and lost the bastard who broke my heart, he gave me a job in his fledgeling estate agency. I love my job. *Really* love it. Sure, it's a bit boring and repetitive – isn't every job? – and yes, I'd liked to have done something more dynamic, but for over ten years it's been my lifeline. And Paul is my lifeguard, watching over me, always there to pick up the pieces when yet another disaster strikes. Which unfortunately it has a habit of doing quite often around me.

I finish off my shopping trip with a visit to Superdrug for basic toiletries and then rush back to the office before my hour is up. No time for a sandwich but my figure probably needs to miss more than just one meal anyway. What my mind needs is work, work and more work, to keep it from thinking about the fact that when it's time to go home tonight, I have no home to go to.

My regular job, since the office expanded last year, is to handle the rentals. This mainly involves dealing with complaints from tenants, anything from 'My tap is dripping' to 'Part of an aeroplane has fallen through the roof'. (It happens, believe me.) Every phone call I get today has me biting my tongue. 'Oh really,' I want to say. 'Well, at least you haven't lost all your possessions in a house fire! How would you feel about that?'

I hold it together, just. Loretta stays out of my way for the rest of the day. At a quarter to five, Joe appears at my desk looking sheepish.

'Hey, Stella,' he says, 'if you're staying here a while I could do with having these details typed up. They need to go out tomorrow.' He holds out his Dictaphone and fixes me with puppy dog eyes.

'Give it here. And don't say I never do anything for you.'

Fitting my earpiece to the machine I press play and begin to type, albeit with only two fingers. Joe's a bit work-shy but his euphemisms and descriptions always make me laugh.

Like this one: "The garden is deceptively small and would appeal to an agoraphobic midget." Not very PC, but Joe, short for Giuseppe (unfortunate phrase, as he is very short indeed), never understands why some of his comments are offensive. This just makes him even funnier, to me at least

"The bathroom is large and green. Like a swamp."

Classic. I type: *Compact easy maintenance garden. Unusually spacious bathroom with avocado suite and scope for further improvement.* It doesn't take long to pick up the spiel in this business.

Most of the homes we sell wouldn't get anywhere near their true value, or sell this side of the next millennium, without a bit of creative marketing.

Judging by Joe's comments, this house is going to need a lot of creative marketing. In one of Milton Keynes' less desirable areas – what we like to call "up and coming" – it has been rented and systematically run down by a succession of tenants from hell. The landlord has obviously given up doing repairs and decided to cut his losses instead.

I look at the pictures and my heart goes out to the poor house – it doesn't look so very different from mine in its current state. Two of the windows are boarded up, the garden's full of rubbish and the front door hangs off its hinges as though kicked in. All it needs is a bit of TLC, but it will probably be bought by another developer who'll pay for basic repairs only and then let it out again to more tenants from hell. If only I had the money …

I pull myself back to reality. No point in thinking that way. I don't even have the money to do up my own wreck of a house, let alone invest in someone else's. I feel a knot of dread in my stomach. It keeps coming back to me like a bad dream – everything I owned disappearing in a cloud of smoke and a torrent of grubby water. If there's a silver lining here I really can't see it.

Just before seven, Paul returns to the office with a huge smile and a spring in his step. I am staring blankly into space and I jump as though shot when he bursts through the door.

'What are you still doing here? Aren't you going home?' he asks.

'Is that supposed to be funny?' I snap. Now, where did that come from? It's not Paul's fault. Win friends, Stella, don't alienate them. 'Sorry,' I tell him, glad to see the hurt look on his face disappear as quickly as it arrived.

'I sold Shenley Church End,' he tells me happily.

'What, the whole district? That's impressive!'

'No, silly.' He gives me a light punch on the arm and I pretend to fall off my chair; an old routine of ours.

'I've sold that house in Shenley Church End. I was starting to despair, this is only the second person I've shown it to and we've had it on for eight months. But he loved it, made an offer there and then. Cash buyer.'

'The best kind.'

'You know it. I called the vendors and that was that. Job done.' He does a little dance across the carpet as I pull up the details on my computer.

'Six bed executive with outbuildings and paddock. Very nice. Although I'm assuming his wife hasn't seen it yet? She may put the kybosh on it, say the feng shui is all wrong. Or the grass in the paddock isn't right for their darling little pony.'

'Stella is a grump, Stella is a grump,' Paul sings, spinning me round in my chair.

I regain my balance and say, somewhat huffily, 'Might I remind you that as I have just lost my own humble abode I'm hardly likely to take great pleasure in the purchase of Holly Bush Heights by Mr and Mrs Rich-and-Important.'

'The business needs this, Stella.' Paul flops down into Joe's empty chair. 'A sold sign on a house like that, well, you can't buy that kind of advertising.'

'I'm really happy for you, boss. You're very *smart*, Mr Smart.'

He looks at me, tilting his head down to meet my eyes, suddenly serious. 'I know it's been tough for you today, Stella, and I can't imagine what you're going through. But I want you to know that I'm proud of you. I think you're handling it all brilliantly. I just know you'll think of something and work it all out. You always do.'

I give him a weak smile. Wish I had his faith. Wish Lipsy had his faith.

Paul is studying me again. 'You look nice.'

'Thanks.' I've changed into the jeans and chiffon top, and it is a definite improvement on too-tight gym clothes.

'Hey, why don't we go out for dinner? I can drop you back here to pick up your car after.'

'Ah, well. My car's not here actually. I got a lift in from my mum.'

'Well, that's ok. I'll drop you back at your mum's.'

'The thing is, I've kind of got a date. Sort of. Not really a date.' I avoid meeting his eyes, which are maddeningly intense right now. 'It's just my next-door neighbour. He feels sorry for me, is all. I'm not that bothered but I said I'd go. It's no big deal.'

'Clearly,' he says, giving me a look that I can't interpret. 'Is this the neighbour who drives a red Mazda and wears his hair slicked back like an Italian football player?'

'That's him! Do you know him?'

'He's outside. You'd better go, he's been waiting for five minutes and he doesn't look the type who likes to wait.'

I throw Paul a sheepish smile as I dash out, but he's already looked away. I turn on my best "date" smile for Mr Waitrose – sorry, *Joshua* is his name, as I found out only yesterday – who leans across the seat to fling open the passenger door. With a backward glance towards the office window, I wonder what I am letting myself in for. And I wonder whether a meal with Paul – comfortable, safe, reliable Paul – would not have been a better prospect.

21

Chapter 3

Paul

Paul pushed the door closed with his foot, hung his jacket on the single hook and threw the mail on the coffee table. His briefcase followed, landing on the sofa. He remembered Stella ribbing him mercilessly when he'd first come into work with that briefcase – soft leather, canvas handle, what she had called a "man bag".

'If anything it's an attaché case,' Paul had countered, slightly bemused at the giggling and sly nods that were coming from his staff.

'Of course it is, Paul,' Stella said, trying to keep a straight face.

'But everyone's got one now. They're in all the shops and besides, it's really useful. Why should it only be women who get to use a bag?' Paul had looked to Joe for support.

'You're right, boss,' said Joe in a tone of voice that suspiciously matched Stella's. 'And very macho it is too.'

Paul had given his new briefcase a few searching looks for the rest of the day but carried on using it regardless. What did he care what people thought?

Especially Stella. He shook his head and smiled to himself as he walked through to the kitchen. If anyone's house was going to burn down it was hers. Calamity followed her around like a stalker. Still, Paul felt genuinely sorry for her this time – she didn't deserve a blow like this. Although the insurance lapse was bad news. Paul couldn't imagine forgetting something as important as that.

But Stella was a fighter and he knew she'd be OK. Look how she'd brought Lipsy up on her own after that loser had dumped her so badly – she was one of the strongest women he'd ever met.

On the other hand, what kind of person arranged a date with a stranger within hours of their house burning down? Nobody normal, that was for sure. Paul shook his head again, turned on the radio, and pulled a beer from the fridge.

When the phone rang, he half expected it to be Stella, her date gone wrong, wanting to be picked up from somewhere or just needing a shoulder to cry on.

'Hi, Paul, it's Loretta.'

Paul sighed. It was great that Loretta was such a conscientious employee, but he wished she wouldn't call him at home so often.

'What's up?' he asked, aiming for disinterested, coming out flat.

'I hope I haven't disturbed you. I was just a bit worried about the sales figures for this month and I needed to talk to you. Perhaps if you're not busy I could come over …'

Paul looked at the phone in horror. 'I'm, erm, I'm just about to go out. Sorry. If it really can't wait until tomorrow I suppose you could just tell me now.'

Good one, he thought, as Loretta launched into a detailed explanation of how everyone in the office wasn't giving her the information she needed. Why couldn't he be more assertive and just tell the woman it would have to wait until tomorrow? If it was Joe he would say exactly that. But women were so unpredictable. He had thought when he promoted her to sales supervisor that it might stop this constant worrying, but if anything it had made her worse. There always seemed to be some crisis – and once again Stella was at the centre of it.

'I've asked her over and over again for the month-end

figures but she just ignores me,' Loretta whined. 'Today she said that I should be worrying about a different kind of figure! Can you believe that?'

Paul stifled a laugh, turned it into a cough, and made sympathetic noises into the receiver. Stella was incorrigible. There was no love lost between these two but Loretta could give as good as she got.

He placated Loretta as best he could, then pretended there was someone at the door and ended the call. It was no wonder he was still single. The only time he had tried dating seriously – a sweet, unchallenging beautician from Bletchley – well, look how badly that had turned out.

No. Friends were so much easier. Friends like Nick and Steve and Jimmy, who he'd known since university and who could sit with him in the pub for hours and talk about absolutely nothing; or Andy, Ethan and Tommo, his Wednesday Poker night buddies, who would roll in the door with a complete lack of expectations and nothing but a bit of innocent gambling on their minds.

And Stella, of course. She was the only woman he had ever been truly comfortable with, but that was only because there was absolutely no romantic involvement at all. His mates were openly jealous of his friendship with her. None of them could quite believe that he didn't secretly fancy her.

'But she's gorgeous,' Steve had said the first time he met her. Paul had shrugged off his friend's teasing; he knew it was a common belief that a man couldn't be friends with a woman without wanting to go to bed with her.

It had made him more protective of her, fielding Steve's 'I'll have a crack at her then if you're not going to' with a forced smile and a resolve to keep her far away his other mates. In a way, she was like the younger sister he didn't have, and he guessed she thought of him as a brother. She didn't seem to have much luck with the opposite sex either. Paul certainly didn't think her latest beau was a likely candidate. He pictured her getting into the red sports car earlier. She didn't even know this neighbour properly. She was vulnerable right now, might be prone to making snap decisions, judgement impaired. Who *was* this guy? Talk about taking advantage...

Give it up, Paul, he told himself. Stella could look after herself and besides, it's not as if she really *was* his sister.

He picked up the phone again and dialled Nick's number. Sod the paperwork – a lads' night out was what he needed. No stress, no worries, no hassle.

***

Stella

As dates go it isn't the worst I've ever had. I can tell that Joshua is trying his best to put me at ease, like when he says he doesn't mind that my blouse clashes horribly with his car. He is joking, I think. And he tries hard to take my mind off my problems, telling me about a friend of his who also lost everything in a house fire. I listen intently. I'd dearly like to know how it played out.

His friend killed himself.

Ah.

The fact that Joshua is very good looking cannot be denied. He is also incredibly knowledgeable and seems to enjoy telling me what food to order and which wine to drink with it. This is fine by me as I'm having trouble deciding when to go to the toilet at the moment. I *need* a bit of guidance.

When we've finished eating, he tells me about his job, something to do with pharmaceuticals. He is very, very passionate about his work. Which is also fine by me; I like a man with a bit of passion. All in all, an effortless night. Joshua doesn't ask me any questions about myself or my work or my family, and as my life feels like it's in shreds at the moment, I enjoy having a night off from myself.

My heart's not in it, though. I try to hide this from Joshua.

26

I'm sure there are many women who'd give anything to go out with him, but I've lived next door to the man for six months and never had him down as dating material. At least, not for me. For Bonnie, maybe. Which is why I wasn't surprised when I saw them talking on the afternoon of the fire. It crossed my mind *briefly* that it was a bit mercenary of Bonnie to hijack my personal tragedy and get off with Mr Smooth, but I wouldn't have held it against her. I *was* surprised when she informed me later that she'd actually been setting him up for a date with me.

Of all the nerve. But bless her for trying.

He insists on having me home by ten o'clock. (Not home, of course, just back to my mum's.) I can tell he's impressed by the house but decide not to invite him in. I wait for that awkward end-of-date moment, half hoping he won't try to kiss me, half hoping he will if only to prove I'm not desperately unattractive.

It is a very long time since I've been out on a date.

Joshua thanks me for a nice evening (nice?) and tells me that I need as much sleep as possible at the moment to be able to cope with what lies ahead. This is touching but also a little unsettling. Is he thinking of his suicide friend again? Before I can analyse this further he leans towards me. Here it comes. But no, he is only reaching across me to fling open the passenger door.

'Night, Stella.'

I get out with as much dignity as the low-to-the-ground sports car will allow and turn to wave as he speeds away.

'Night, Joshua,' I say to the empty street.

Inside the house, I creep up to my room and close the door softly. I am under strict instructions to call Bonnie the minute I get in. But first I fight with the urge to check on Lipsy. She hates it when I do what she calls "smothering" and I call "mothering". I didn't really *want* to go out tonight – I felt I should be here for my daughter. But, as Bonnie said, what was the point? Lipsy can't stand the sight of me at the moment. The best thing I can do for her is to stay out of her way.

I comfort myself by pressing my ear firmly to her bedroom door. The familiar irregular thump and grind of her favourite hip-hop music reassures me and I tiptoe back to my room.

Bonnie answers on the first ring.

'I'm sorry to disappoint you but there's nothing to report,' I tell her.

'He didn't try to kiss you even?'

'Nope.'

'Oh. What a shame.' She sounds as disappointed as if it had been her own date.

'He hardly looked at me in that way, to be honest. I must be losing my touch, along with everything else.'

'Come on Stella, don't get down about it. He's just being a gentleman. He's bound to treat you with kid gloves after what's happened.'

'Yeah, I guess.' I bet Bonnie wouldn't have this problem. She'd have to fight him off with a stick. 'I shouldn't have gone, Bonnie. It was a total waste of time. And Lipsy probably thinks I've deserted her, and my mother will give me the third degree in the morning.' I think about the expression on Paul's face earlier. 'How do you think it looks to people, going out on dates when your house just burnt down?' I catch my voice before it turns into a wail.

Bonnie sighs heavily like I'm a small, annoying child. 'The Stella Hill *I* know doesn't care what other people think. You went out for dinner with a neighbour, so what? It's not even as if you can cook your own, now you haven't got a kitchen anymore.' She has a point there. 'And besides,' she says bracingly, 'your house didn't burn down, Stella. It's damaged, it's a lot the worse for wear, and it's pretty soggy, but it is still there. It's still standing.'

I roll my eyes. Still standing, but only just. OK on the outside but gutted on the inside, needing a hell of a lot of love

28

and attention to put it even halfway right.

Now, who does that remind me of?

'I've been thinking,' Bonnie says. 'What you need is a plan. A "Get Your House In Order" plan. And I want you to start by making a list of what you need to do to get back on track. You know, things you need to sort out, stuff to buy.' She pauses for a second. 'I mean important things, Stella, not just the stuff you'd like to have, not a bigger telly or a bigger and better sound system.'

Insulted, I glare into the phone. How dare she?

As Bonnie drones on I look at my watch. Maybe Joshua was right and I should get an early night. Tomorrow I plan to be very brave and make a visit to Chaplin Grove to check out the damage.

'Bonnie, I'd better go. I need to get some sleep. You know, big day tomorrow and all that.'

'Write the list,' she screeches in my ear as I hang up.

Lists! Bonnie is obsessed with lists. She makes lists of the lists she has to write every week. I, on the other hand, prefer to wing it. Usually. Although I have to admit, this is an unusual circumstance.

My mother has put one of her nightdresses on my pillow – brushed cotton with long sleeves and big blue flowers. With a sigh I undress and pull it over my head, sitting down heavily on the bed. My childhood bed, with its saggy centre and spindly legs.

There is no way I can sleep. This will be my third night of staring at the walls, going over and over all the mistakes I've made until I want to take my mum's nightdress and hang myself with it. My eyes feel too big for their sockets and every time I try to close them my eyelids snap open like they're on elastic.

I sit against the pillows and pick up a book, a teenage favourite of mine, Nancy Drew. The words blur together. After a few minutes, I throw it to the floor in disgust.

Bonnie's suggestion comes back to me and I consider it. A

list of all the things I need, she said. It's a daunting prospect but why not? I have to start somewhere. In a drawer, I find sheets of paper – pale pink with balloons up the side – and a chewed blue biro. Perfect.

Sitting at my childhood desk, far too tall for it now, knees knocking against it every time I move, I stare at the paper for a long time. I don't know where to start. Easier to write a list of what I *do* have left than what I don't. That list would be a lot shorter.

I resolve to be positive. If Lipsy can handle it OK – and she seems to be coping much better than I am – then I can make the effort too. The house will be fixed up and redecorated and I will replace everything we've lost with stuff that is bigger and better (or smaller and better), and I'll be happier than ever before. Maybe Lipsy could help me do up the house, kind of like a bonding exercise for us. That could work. I will pay off all my debts and find a great man who idolizes me. (I think I'm on to a loser with Joshua but I can't afford to be too fussy right now.) I tuck my legs under the desk, wincing as I scrape my knees again, and grip the pen resolutely in my hand. I touch it to the top of the page and begin to write:

CAN'T LIVE WITHOUT ...

Chapter 4

Stella

It looks like the latest Damien Hurst installation dropped into suburbia. Luckily for them, the houses on either side of mine are completely untouched; though they're detached, the spaces in between are only just about wide enough to walk through sideways.

I pick my way along the path, pull aside the makeshift boarded door and enter a world of darkness. This can't be the same house, I think to myself, shaking my head in wonder. It can't be the house I've lived in with my beautiful daughter for thirteen years. The house I decorated lovingly in apple green and duck egg blue, came home to every night, good days, bad days, always there to welcome me with a glass of chilled Pinot Grigio. I have a vision that *my* house has been beamed up by aliens and replaced by this impostor as some kind of cruel cosmic joke. Somewhere, in a galaxy far away, little grey men are sitting around my kitchen table laughing their oversized grey heads off and drinking my wine.

The smell that hits me as I cross the threshold is stale and musty like a house that's been abandoned for months, not days. Three steps take me into the lounge, and I wait for my eyes to adjust after the morning sunlight. Only a little of that light creeps through the filthy windows. Every visible surface is a sooty, dirty brown, and there is nothing familiar to be seen.

The floating sensation I had on Saturday envelops me again. When I last came in here, only a few hours after the fire had finally been put out, a fireman tried to warn me what to expect. He'd said that the heat and smoke damage were extensive. And then there was the water. The damage from the water was almost as bad as the damage from the fire itself. He even gave me a booklet, *Recovering From Your Fire or Flood*, which Bonnie read from cover to cover. Twice. She also went out and bought a disposable camera and told me to take photographs of the damage. I didn't know where to start.

But that was when she thought I had insurance, of course. Without it, there was no reason to record the devastation. I took photos anyway and hoped that one day I could put them side by side with photos of a shiny new house and feel proud of what I'd achieved, and of how well I'd coped.

I wasn't coping very well now.

My house is of the small two-bedroomed variety common in Milton Keynes. Downstairs there's a lounge-dining room with French windows at one end and a window overlooking the cul-de-sac at the other, a kitchen and a cloakroom – or downstairs loo, as my mother calls it. Upstairs: two bedrooms and a bathroom.

I pick my way through to the kitchen, once my pride and joy. Cath Kidston eat your heart out. Pink and blue, bunting and kitsch curtains, my beautiful – if rarely used – Kenwood mixer on the counter. And my wonderful, show-stopping, American fridge-freezer with ice maker and enough room to freeze a dead body or two.

To say the room is unrecognisable is the understatement of the year. Everywhere my eyes rest gives up a new horror, from the blistered, peeling paintwork to the twisted remains of the fridge. And everything is a damp, dull brown.

A glint of light in the corner catches my eye, and I step carefully over the debris to reach it. It is the remains of a glass mosaic candle holder, made from blue and green squares, a gift from my mother. Now it's covered in soot like everything else, and the glass has been bent out of shape by the heat.

Funny, I've never really admired the thing before. It was just there, just another ornament. I don't think I've ever even bothered to put a candle in it. But suddenly, vividly, I remember how the sun used to flood in through the window and cause the mosaic glass to fling beautiful coloured patterns across the wall.

The thought makes me unbearably sad.

I stumble backwards, catching my bare ankle on a sharp piece of wood sticking out from the remains of my kitchen table. I cry out as it tears through the thin skin. Pain shoots up my leg. As if this fire hasn't done enough damage, now the remains of it are attacking me.

'Stupid thing!' somebody shrieks. (I think it might be me.)

I kick the table hard, sending black soot flying across the room. A sound throbs in my head like a heartbeat, pounding against my ears, and it drowns out the noises I make as I crash about the room, venting a sudden fit of anger. I kick at the nearest kitchen cupboard, reducing it to splinters and ashes. I lash out at the twisted frame of the microwave, and it falls to the floor with a satisfying crash.

The release feels good in a weird, unhealthy way, and I attack whatever I can reach, wanting to destroy it all. Perhaps I need to put my own stamp on it again, take back the power from the fire. My fury takes me out of the kitchen and into the lounge, where I attack the remains of my sofa, my fists thumping uselessly at the waterlogged fabric.

Most of the furniture is sodden and heavy with water. The soot I dislodge flies up into my face and sticks to my tears. I breathe it in and it sticks in my throat, making me cough.

Eventually, I wear myself out.

Stop in the middle of the room, panting loudly.

Become aware of someone standing in the doorway, watching me.

Joshua.

Terrific.

'Oh, hi!' I say, as if thrashing around a disaster zone on a Tuesday afternoon in June is totally normal behaviour.

Joshua stares at me suspiciously out of those impossibly deep brown eyes. 'I heard noises. I thought someone had broken in.'

'Like someone would,' I answer, sarcastically. 'It's not as if there's anything to steal.'

'Kids, I mean,' Joshua says, smoothing his hair back with both hands, a habit I'd noticed on our date last night. 'What are you doing?'

'Oh, you know. Just surveying the damage. Seeing if there's anything salvageable before the decorators move in.' As you might have guessed, I have kept the small matter of insurance secret.

Joshua nods sagely. 'Very wise,' he says, and then he stuns me by asking me out to dinner again.

I hear myself saying yes before my brain has had a chance to think it through properly. I guess it's just that there haven't been so many offers in the last few years that I feel comfortable turning down someone who is, if a little odd, at least very eligible. When you're a single mum – especially when you're a single mum who's a bit past it, as Lipsy likes to tell me – men tend to be thin on the ground. The only ones who notice you exist are either harassed single dads looking for some help with the kids or desperate bachelors on the lookout for a ready-made family. Only, they're not so keen on the ready-made variety that comes with a stroppy seventeen-year-old who has serious issues with her frazzled mum. Not in my humble experience, anyway.

Joshua tells me he's busy for the rest of the week but can make it next Monday evening. I nod vaguely, my attention wandering back to the state of my walls. When he finally leaves me to it, I plonk myself down in the middle of the floor to think.

From my battered holdall I extract the list I started last night. There are only two items on it so far and I'm too

34

embarrassed to tell you what they are. (OK! An American double-door ice-maker fridge-freezer and a Kenwood food mixer. Happy now?) Bonnie told me to think of important things that I really need, and I figure this is a reasonable start, but possibly not what she had in mind...

Shaking out the pink sheet of paper I smooth it onto my lap and, pen in hand, try again. Think, Stella, think. Well, I'm going to need furniture. Lots of it. And clothes, of course. Proper clothes, not this capsule nonsense. Stuff for Lipsy. I brush my sooty hair out of my eyes and start to scribble:

CAN'T LIVE WITHOUT
American double-door ice-maker fridge-freezer
Kenwood food mixer
Furniture! (Sofa, dining table, chairs, beds,
*   wardrobes ...)*
Clothes: see sub-list
TV
Lipsy - computer, Playstation, iPod, clothes ...

Oh my God, this is a huge amount of stuff. It's impossible to think that I'll ever be able to pay for it all on my tiny salary. And my chances of getting a loan are slimmer than a Hollywood A-lister – my credit rating isn't exactly what you would call "prime". Feeling panicked all over again, I rack my brains for anybody I could ask for a loan.

My poor brain comes up empty. Bonnie's reasonably well-off but I wouldn't want to put our friendship under the kind of strain that borrowing money might engender. Ditto Paul. My brother, Billy, is broke as far as I know – and nobody knows where he is anyway. Which just leaves my mum, and that's a complete non-starter. Lately, she's had a bit of a blow in the income department. Namely that her one source of income, my father, has been temporarily removed.

And he's definitely not in a position to lend me money.

No, I don't want to talk about my father. I don't visit, I don't write, and, if I can help it, I don't talk about him at all.

To anyone.

Especially not my mother.

* * *

Later that day I am curled up on my mother's sofa watching *Calamity Jane*. After a stressful few hours at the house, I decided to finish my afternoon off with some quiet time watching a classic. My mother is off doing what she does best – shopping – and Lipsy is out with her new boyfriend. This boyfriend was news to me but my mother knows all about it and seems to approve. Not sure if I should be reassured by or worried about this.

Alistair the lodger is at work being slimy and I have the whole house to myself. It feels great. *Calamity Jane* on TV is a bonus, and for once I am benefiting from my mum's exorbitantly expensive taste. The sofa is soft, the television flat-screen and huge, the duvet made from the feathers of the finest baby ducks.

My father built this house in Shenley Church End during the early days of Milton Keynes' development, when his construction firm was raking it in and land prices were still relatively low. It looks grand and impressive if you like that sort of thing. Five bedrooms, two receptions, study, double garage, etc. "Executive Homes" we call them at Smart's.

He indulged my mum in everything, and as a result, the décor is a showy blend of bad taste and no taste. I will grudgingly admit that my father was generous. I have to: he bought my house for Lipsy and me when my daughter was three and I was desperate. Although, I was never sure whether he only bought it because he just couldn't stand all the noise and the mess at home any longer.

But I don't want to talk about him.

Just at the point when Doris Day reveals to the man of her dreams that she scrubs up quite well, I hear the front door open. Bugger, my favourite bit ruined. I look at the clock. It is just after four and I deduce from this that my mother is returning home. How you ask? No way on earth she'll miss *Deal Or No Deal*. She adores Noel Edmunds. Well, somebody has to.

I gather up my duvet and creep out of the lounge, hoping to make it to the stairs without being discovered. No such luck.

'Stella! What a lovely surprise, you're home already. Oh sweetie, are you not well?'

She drops her bags on the parquet floor and rushes over to put a hand on my forehead. Why do mums do that? I swat it away and glare at the bags.

'I thought you were broke. Where'd you get the money to buy all this stuff?'

'Don't be angry, Stella,' she pleads. 'I know I shouldn't have but I couldn't resist. Look, this was such a bargain, half price.'

The object she holds out is so hideous I physically recoil.

'Urghh, what the hell is it?'

Little black eyes stare malevolently out of a shiny round face. (That's the ornament, not my mother.)

'Well, anyway,' she puts the offending item away – half china dog, half Chucky the killer doll – and produces a heap of fluffy baby-blue fabric from yet another bag. 'I bought you a present too, sweetie.' Hands it to me.

'Thanks.' Jesus, haven't I suffered enough already?

'They're pyjamas,' she tells me.

'I can see that.'

'They weren't expensive. And you lost the ones I bought you for Christmas in, you know, the *fire*.'

This she whispers as if I could be physically burnt by the word *fire*.

The last lot of pyjamas she bought for me had gone the way of all the others long before the fire – to the charity shop – but I say a dutiful thank you and give her the insisted upon kiss. I have so few clothes I can't afford to be fussy, and I am quite touched. They probably were expensive, as she would never shop anywhere cheap, and the fact that she's spent money on me that she could have spent on herself is nice. Although, then you have to consider that she has no money of her own and everything she spends goes on credit cards – credit cards that I will probably end up having to pay off for her. Then the generosity pales a little.

'It's quarter past four! Come and watch *Deal Or No Deal* with me, Stella.'

That I *can* live without.

I make an excuse and retreat upstairs.

Only to find myself pacing around aimlessly like a caged sloth. My eighteen-year-old self stares back at me via posters, books and keepsakes. I know that under the bed I will find a box of cards and letters from old boyfriends and on top of the yellow-pine wardrobe my old record collection: early acid house, Salt-n-Pepa, Duran Duran. The shame!

My door is slightly open, and when I hear noises on the landing I press my nose to the gap. Lipsy and a person I can only assume is her new boyfriend are creeping along the corridor towards her room, hand in hand, stifling giggles. As I'd only heard of his existence a few days ago, you'll understand that I want to have a good look. I make my eye big and peer at them from behind the safety of the door.

The boy is taller than my daughter by a good six inches, but then she is a little mite. He has that fine wispy hair that always makes a bloke look younger until he loses it, then he ages really quickly. Lipsy has her face close to his and I don't think I've ever seen her look so beautiful. I feel sorry for them and jealous of them all at the same time. Her bedroom door closes softly and I smile to myself for a moment.

A very brief moment. Something about that picture was wrong and it takes a few more seconds before it sinks in.

That wasn't a boy going into my seventeen-year-old daughter's bedroom. Not some pimply youth interested in Playstation games and football. That person was most definitely a *man*.

I stream across the corridor and burst into her room, knocking both of them flying as I do – serves them right for leaning against the door in a clinch. How dare he? He stands in front of Lipsy as if protecting her from some mad woman, not as tall as I thought and certainly no oil painting. Oh yes, I bet he thought all his Christmases had come at once when he met my daughter.

'Mum!' Lipsy pushes him out of the way and steps up to bar my progress. 'What the hell do you think you're doing? This is my room, get out.'

I take a step back and reach behind me for the door handle. I need support.

'Just what do you think you're doing, madam? Who the hell is this MAN? And what is he doing in your bedroom?'

'This,' says Lipsy, a look of total unconcern on her face, 'is Robert. Rob to his friends, so you can call him Robert. He's my boyfriend. And now, if you don't mind, we're busy.'

With that she gives me a hearty shove and shuts – and locks! – the door in my face.

For a moment or two, I can't breathe. I think I might suffocate right here on the landing. Then, recovering enough to raise a fist, I begin to bang ferociously on her door.

'Get. Out. Here. Now.'

'What's all the noise?' My mother has come to join in the fun and I round on her, remembering that she knew all about this and did nothing.

'Do you know how old this boyfriend is?' I demand.

She looks slightly perturbed as if she's being asked to remember the name of an actor from a show in the seventies.

'He's old,' I tell her. 'And he's in there with her now. In her bedroom, Mum.'

'Well, now, I don't think he's old. I seem to remember Lipsy saying he was twenty-something.'

She actually says this as though it's helpful.

'Oh well, I don't even know why I was worried. I'll go

back to my own room shall I and forget all about it? ARE YOU INSANE?'

Just then Lipsy's door swings open again and she steps out onto the landing, calmly closing the door behind her.

'Get out here, you cradle-snatcher!' I shout over her shoulder.

'Mum!' My daughter is looking at me with an expression of such disgust it stops my hollering and demands full attention. 'Will you just listen to yourself? Do you really think standing here shouting is going to make any difference to what I do? Rob and I have been seeing each other for months and there is nothing you can do about it. Nothing!' she insists as I try to protest. 'Anyway, Grandma is happy for me to have him here and it's her house and not yours.'

The "so there" element to her voice is so young and innocent I am tempted to start my protesting anew. But, as ever, I can see the futility of the task. I could shout and scream and create. I could maybe drag the man out of her room by his scrawny neck and throw him bodily down the stairs. I could (try to) lock her in her room in an attempt to teach her a lesson. But with Lipsy, these things just never seem to work. Believe me, I've tried them. I guess it's my failing as her mother that I never found quite the right way to discipline her, never mastered the art of making her do what I say simply because I say it.

Instead, I decide to attack my mother, who was far too good at being strict with me to be letting Lipsy get away with this now. 'Is this right?' I demand of her. 'Are you   OK with this happening in your house?'

My mother stands between us, her face creased with confusion. She looks from me to Lipsy and back again. I hear movements from behind the door to my daughter's bedroom and wonder what the man, what Robert, is doing.

'Well, the thing is, I can't really say… that is, I'm not sure that it's …'

'Oh, don't bother.' I turn away from the pair of them so

they can't see the tears of frustration that are starting to puddle in my eyes. As I reach for the door to my room – my own teenage bedroom where, God knows, I got up to stuff I fervently pray Lipsy will never do – my daughter throws out her killer blow.

'You're such a hypocrite, Mum. After all, you weren't that much older than me when you got pregnant.'

Chapter 5

Lipsy

Wednesday 6th June

I hate my mother.

As of today the above statement is official and nothing she can do will ever change my mind.

Yesterday the woman formerly known as my mother went totally ballistic when she found Rob in my room. She caused a scene like you would not believe. I was so ashamed. Thankfully Rob was cool about it but afterwards he said he didn't feel right doing it with her in the house. Just great!

Then, as if she hadn't done enough already, she goes and phones my dad, who we never see anyway, and tells him all about it. Like he gives a shit. But that made everything ten million times worse because for the past six months I've been telling my mum that I was staying at my dad's at weekends when I kind of wasn't. I was actually staying with Rob.

Now I'm grounded. Grandma is backing her up so that's it. My life's over. Rob will meet someone else – that Nina at McDonald's likes him, I'm sure. And she's got blonde hair and she's such a tart ...

No. Must not worry. Rob isn't like that. And if he is then it will be all my mother's fault and I'll make her pay forever.

Lipsy snapped her diary shut and returned it to its secret

43

place under her mattress. Lately, she'd been filling it with the kind of things she had a feeling should not be viewed by anyone else but her. And her mum had turned into such a pain in the arse she wouldn't put it past her to sneak around looking for evidence against her.

No, it was safer to keep it well and truly hidden. Maybe she should think of some kind of code for certain things; she knew that was what her friend Rosie did in her diary. Rosie had explained the code to Lipsy, which Lipsy thought was a bit stupid – what was the point of a secret code if your best friend knew how to break it?

Still, she was grateful for the advice. She needed all the weapons she could find against her mother now. It was all-out war.

***

Paul

Paul stirred two sugars into his latte, rolling his eyes in disgust as the hot liquid slopped over into the plate-sized saucer. Never mind that these trendy coffee shops had to give you your drink in a cup the size of a soup bowl, did they have to fill them right to the brim? And look at the handle on the mug – too small for even a child's finger to fit through. He hated these places, full of frazzled shoppers and self-conscious types. He could have told Stella no, he'd meet her somewhere else, like the pub for example, but he knew Café Crème was her favourite hangout.

Lifting the mug carefully to his lips, he sipped the scalding liquid and watched the door closely. A tall woman with dark hair appeared behind a group of rowdy teenagers and Paul stretched his head to see. It wasn't Stella. When she did arrive she would be full of life, immediately telling him about some scrape she'd had on the way into town or a near-miss in the car park, always some drama. He couldn't believe how well she'd coped this week. She was amazing. Paul didn't even want to think how he'd feel if he lost everything he owned – without insurance, as well. But Stella had breezed into the office on Wednesday morning, the energy fairly bursting out of her, and happily announced that she was going to do up her house herself and make it even better than it was before.

She'd need a lot of help, though. Paul had sat her down during her lunch break and made her start on a list of jobs that needed doing. He thought he was being constructive and was taken aback when she rolled her eyes and said, 'Oh for God's sake, not another list!'

But, like any good friend, he'd offered his services, and – possibly more usefully – the services of the handyman Smart Homes used for all its maintenance jobs. Stella's eyes had filled with tears at this point, but Paul had shrugged off her thanks. It was the least he could do.

Two young women were looking at him across the café, their heads together conspiratorially and their faces arranged into surreptitious smiles. It took Paul a few minutes to realise that they were smiling at him. He felt his face grow hot and he looked away, embarrassed. He was just no good at this kind of thing. He knew if Steve or Nick were here now they'd be egging him on to go and ask for phone numbers, and he knew that no matter how much they pressured him he simply wouldn't be able to do it.

What was wrong with a man being in his late thirties and still single? He was perfectly happy, thank you very much, and resented the implication by everyone from his friends to his parents to magazines and TV that it should be any different. His life was full – fuller than most of the couples he knew who did nothing more exciting than watch telly every night, their routine punctuated only by the odd drink-fuelled argument. Who wanted routine and commitment and – perish the thought – kids, anyway?

As if in punishment, a woman with a buggy wide enough for triplets barged roughly past his seat. In a considerate reflex, Paul tried to jerk it out of the way. And spilt half his coffee into his lap. Thankfully, he'd been gazing into space for so long the temperature was only on the hot side of warm. Otherwise – he didn't want to think about otherwise. The woman squeezed by him and glared, looking pointedly at his lap.

'It's only coffee,' Paul tried to explain but she'd already gone, threading around the tables like a rally driver.

'Had a bit of an accident?'

Stella stood over him, smirking as he dabbed at the stain with a soggy napkin.

'Very funny.' Paul tried to smile but the humour of the situation was, for once, lost on him. His ruminations had left him feeling defensive, and he wondered whether he should have talked to those two women after all. Too late now. 'Sit down, I'll get you a coffee. Oh. You've already got one.'

'I've been here ages. I was in the queue trying to catch your eye. You look like a man with a lot on his mind, you were miles away. Anything I should know?'

'Nothing important. Muffin?' he said, pushing the bag of mini-muffins across the table.

'No thanks, I'm watching my figure.'

'Don't worry, I'll watch it for you,' he countered, to which Stella responded with a hearty laugh. Paul began to relax again. He knew she loved this kind of banter, and he loved the way that she could take it without getting snitty or precious like some women. Or take it too seriously, like some other women.

Despite the joke – or maybe because of it – he found himself looking at her figure as she sat back, coffee in hand, and thinking how perfect it was. Long legs – not skinny, just right. Trim waist. Great-shaped body dipping in and out in all the right places – ALL the right places. He wasn't sure when exactly she'd turned from the gangly, sweet kid at school into the voluptuous woman who sat before him now, and he wondered why he had never noticed it before.

Because she's a friend, Smart, he told himself sternly, annoyed at the way he'd caught himself acting like the kind of man he couldn't stand. What sort of a bloke leers at their friends? Particularly vulnerable friends like Stella. It must be his age, and the constant pressure from some invisible source to abandon his bachelor lifestyle.

He resolved to make it up to her by giving her a pay rise. God knows, she deserved it.

'What's up with you, Smart-boy? You're doing that staring into space thing again?' Stella prodded him with her spoon.

Paul shook himself mentally. Snap out of it, man. 'I'm good,' he said. 'How about you?'

'Not good.' Stella smiled ruefully. 'I've had a really bad morning, to be honest.'

'Lipsy?'

'You guessed it.' She leant forward with her elbows on the table. 'You know, I can't believe I was such a mug, believing she was staying at her dad's all those weekends. I should have known, shouldn't I? I mean, I know what he's like. I know how little interest he's shown in his daughter, so why was I willing to believe that he'd suddenly started wanting her to stay overnight? He's only got a bedsit! How stupid am I?' Stella shook her head, not noticing that a few strands of hair had settled in her cappuccino. 'Don't answer that. Any normal mother would have seen through it immediately. And then I might have been able to protect her from this Robert character. From getting into something she's just too young to understand.'

Paul reached over and rescued her hair from the coffee. 'You're being too hard on yourself, Stella. You're a great mother, you know you are. Look at what you've been through to provide a good home for the two of you–'

'Oh, yes. I made a great job of that, didn't I? And then I went and burnt it down.'

'You didn't burn it down.'

'But I tell you what,' Stella carried on over him, 'I may be a shit mother but I'm a damn sight better mother than he ever will be a father. He's not going to worm his way back into her life now. Not if I have anything to do with it.'

'What do you mean?'

Stella sat back and stirred her coffee with her finger, then transferred the finger to her mouth and licked off the froth. Paul knew he would find this gesture irresistibly sexy on another woman, someone who wasn't only a friend. He shook the thought away again. Perhaps it was just too damn long since he'd had a date. Maybe that was why he was having these weird thoughts. He glanced over to where the two women had been sitting, but their table was empty. Typical.

'He says he wants to get to know her properly,' Stella said grimly. 'After seventeen years of nothing more than the odd Christmas card, now it seems he does actually want to know his daughter. Which is what I thought he was doing for the last six months. It's as if now he's heard about this Robert he wants to do the father thing. Like I'm not a good mother. Like I've failed. Well, I told him he could whistle.' Stella fixed Paul with a steely glare and he was suddenly very glad that he was not the reviled John Dean. In a voice that could freeze a volcano, she said, 'He's got absolutely no chance.'

Paul would have liked to tell his friend that, really, she had no choice in the matter. She had to let her daughter see her father; if anything she should encourage it. It was the right thing to do. But he didn't. He knew her too well to point out the obvious. The time would come when she'd ask him for advice. Until then he'd be a proper friend and just listen.

Stella carried on raging and Paul allowed himself to listen with half an ear. Mentally, he reviewed his plans for the weekend: coffee with Stella, an afternoon shopping for work clothes, dinner with Steve and his girlfriend later (which hopefully wouldn't involve another cringingly embarrassing attempt to fix him up with one of her workmates), and then squash tomorrow followed by a Sunday afternoon viewing. He didn't mind working on a weekend; in the property business, it had to be done. And Paul consoled himself with the thought that if he did have a girlfriend she wouldn't be too happy about this at all. Yet another reason to be grateful for his fancy-free lifestyle.

He settled back with a smile, watching Stella's face get redder and redder. She was going to give herself a coronary if she wasn't careful. Relationships? No thanks.

***

Stella

Paul is looking at me with an amused expression on his face. As I've just been recounting my long list of grievances against Lipsy's feckless father, I don't think amusement is entirely appropriate. I tell him this in no uncertain terms and am even more pissed off when his smile gets wider.

'What is so bloody funny?' I demand, starting to feel a little hurt now. Normally Paul is right there with me when I indulge in a John Dean hate-fest – he despises the man.

'Nothing,' he says, laughing. 'Just… No, it doesn't matter.'
'Go on! What?'

'I was just thinking, that's all. That relationships aren't all they're cracked up to be, are they? And that I really am very happy being single.'

'Oh, God, me too!' I enthuse quickly. Too quickly – Paul gives me the old raised eyebrow. 'No, I am! Really. I'm happier than I've ever been and I *so* don't have time for a man in my life right now.'

'Right.' Paul nods solemnly. 'So what was that date with your neighbour about the other night?'

He has me there. I have no choice but to come out fighting.

'Just because I go on dates,' (the plural being a gross

exaggeration) 'doesn't mean I'm looking for a *relationship*.' I pause and go for the jugular. 'But at least *I* can get a date.'

The look on Paul's face makes me cringe. I've gone too far. Why am I being such a bitch to him? All he's done this past week is offer huge amounts of support and advice, on everything from my rubbish finances to the rebuilding of my house. And here I am insulting him. Nice going, Stella.

I am about to apologise when Bonnie shows up and the mood lightens considerably. She has this effect, does Bonnie; she's a little ray of Scottish sunshine in Milton Keynes' sometimes gloomy atmosphere.

'Hey you two, who's died?' she says, slipping her frame into a tub chair and setting down a tray piled high with cake, coffee and biscuits. How can such a small person have such a huge appetite?

'How's Marcus?' I ask quickly, steering the subject in a direction loved-up Bonnie can't resist.

'Ah, just great.'

I tell you, she positively glows when she talks about him. If it wasn't for Bonnie, my faith in humanity would have died a long time ago. This woman does everything with such enthusiasm that if you spend enough time with her it can't help but rub off on you.

Bonnie turns her radiance on Paul. 'Last night he surprised me with a special meal. Jamie Oliver eat your heart out, my Marcus is a super-chef. When I came in from work he'd filled the bathroom with candles and run me a bath, scented bubbles and everything. Have you ever heard anything so romantic?'

'No. I can't say that I have,' Paul says, sounding distinctly nonplussed.

All that stuff I just told Paul about being happier than ever before and having no time for a man isn't exactly true, as much as it pains me to admit it. I'd love to have a man like Bonnie's Marcus. Not actually Marcus, you understand, but somebody like him. I wonder why I felt the need to lie to Paul.

I've never kept anything from him before. So why do I suddenly have the urge to present a false front?

Not that I think I convinced him for a minute.

Paul's reaction to Bonnie's romantic little story was so sour I feel the need to try and make up for it. 'Bonnie, that's just so wonderful!' I gush. 'He ran you a bath? With candles and bubbles? I'd love someone to do that for me, I really would.'

We both turn as Paul chokes violently on his latte, and as I'm the closest I reach over to thump him on the back. I only do this because I think it will help, but I guess I've got it confused with getting a fishbone stuck in your throat or something. The look Paul gives me says, yes, I definitely got it wrong.

His face is red with the effort of coughing and I decide he deserves the pain – he is clearly trying to stifle yet another laugh at my expense. I'm thinking of a suitable retort when Bonnie squeals and grabs my arm.

'Marcus is here!' she says, as though she's announcing the second coming.

Paul and I duly turn our attention to the man weaving his way towards us. He has a small boy in tow and they noisily pull up two more chairs, scraping them across the wooden floor in a way that sets my teeth on edge.

'Hey guys, what you up to?' Marcus beams at us and then leans over to give Bonnie an affectionate kiss.

The boy is about eight, and is the snottiest child I have ever seen: chronic rhinitis apparently. Poor kid. He has a tissue permanently clutched in his fist and you have to watch out for the killer sneezes. They can take your toupee off.

'Marcus and I are going to get Cory a birthday present today. Aren't we, Cory?' says Bonnie sweetly. She holds out her hand to ruffle his hair and he promptly sneezes all over it. Atta boy.

Paul stands up suddenly. 'I have to be going too. Nice to see you again, Marcus. Cory.' The three lads shake hands the way men do, even the little boy. So sweet. 'Have a good rest of the day,' Paul says, and then, 'See you, Stella.'

And just like that, he's off. Now, call me a bit thick but when we arranged to meet for coffee I had the distinct impression we were also spending the day together. I distinctly remember the words "shopping" and "lunch" from somewhere in the conversation. Perhaps I imagined it. But before I can say anything he is hot-footing it out of Café Crème as though his arse is on fire. Some friend!

I don't know where the sinking feeling comes from. It's not like I'd been looking forward to seeing him or anything – I see him every day of the week, for goodness sake.

Deciding that I must be more depressed than I realised, I turn to Bonnie and Marcus for help. Maybe they'd like some advice on what to buy an eight-year-old for his birthday. But I can tell immediately that I won't get a look in from that quarter. The three of them are wrapped so tight there's no room in the package for a slightly bored mate with an afternoon free. I am truly happy for Bonnie that she's found a great bloke. I just hope there are one or two left out there for me. Well, just one will do, of course. I'm not greedy.

As Bonnie and her ready-made family disappear into the throngs in the shopping centre, bound for toy shop heaven, I decide to treat myself to another cappuccino. I think I deserve it. I think I'm coping fairly well with everything that's going on at the moment. I have a plan (to renovate my house) and a list (of all the things I can't live without) and I even have a mission (to stop my daughter falling into a pit of teenage sex and depravity). Not bad going for one week.

What I don't have, however, is a scrap of spare cash, and at least two of the above require stacks of it. Or possibly all three, as my daughter is as susceptible to being bought as any seventeen-year-old. What I need is money. Money for paint and rollers and carpets and kitchen units. Money for my ever-increasing debts and my drastically decreased wardrobe. Money, money, money.

What I need is a miracle.

I'm about to pay for my coffee when I notice the sign above the till. "Friendly, outgoing staff wanted for evenings and weekends. Apply within."

Yes! That is it. I will get a job here, at my favourite coffee shop. It won't solve all my problems immediately but it has to be a start. And fate. If Paul hadn't left me here all alone I wouldn't have come back to the counter and I wouldn't have seen the sign. Fate.

Funny thing, fate. I've never really believed in it before. But I guess when you've got virtually nothing left and your life is pretty much in tatters, even the most random thing can seem to have a special meaning. I put on my most engaging smile and ask to see the manager.

Chapter 6

Stella

As I'm creeping down the stairs on Monday morning, trying to get out of the house without being noticed, I hear my mum crying in the kitchen. I pause, freeze-frame style, one hand resting lightly on the banister, all my weight balanced on my left leg. A memory from childhood reminds me that two of the stair treads creak near the bottom, so when I move forward I do so even more carefully. Down the hall, past the dining room, holding my breath and tiptoeing, I try hard to block out the sound of low sobbing.

You may think it heartless, ignoring someone so obviously upset. But I have to. I can't afford to let her into my head at the moment. This very morning I made the mistake of looking at myself in the mirror while I cleaned my teeth (usually I do it by feel alone), and the sight was really quite disturbing. Familiar but strange, like a friend who suddenly reinvents herself and you know she's different but you can't quite work out how.

But in my case, it was the opposite – like being *un*-invented.

I concluded, after much scrutiny, that my life-long policy of trying to avoid emotional problems at all costs was definitely better for my looks and I vowed to return to it immediately. So, you understand, my looks, my health – my entire future happiness – prevent me from going to my mum at this moment.

And I nearly make it out of the house with this intention intact.

Nearly, but not quite.

When I reach the front door I catch an extra loud sob and an involuntary hiccup. Silently cursing my weakness, I turn on my heel and walk calmly back towards the drama.

The kitchen in my parents' house is an overly large farmhouse-style indulgence. My mother sits at the enormous wooden table with her head bowed low, arms stretched in a wide circle as though hugging something. She is dwarfed by the oversized ladder-back chair and looks early-morning rough in her favourite fluffy dressing gown.

She doesn't notice me at first, which gives me time to take in the source of her anguish. As if I didn't know already. She has surrounded herself with photographs: images of the family, staged scenes from long-ago holidays, awkwardly posed pictures of Billy and me as children with fake smiles or genuine frowns. But most of the photographs, unsurprisingly, are of my father.

One picture in particular I have seen her crying over many times before. This one has him frozen in time on the day they met. It is a story she loved to tell us when we were kids, and I remember the faraway glaze that would mist her eyes when she got to her favourite part.

Margaret Foster – known to her friends as Maggie – worked in a bookshop in a pretty village called Stony Stratford, on the outskirts of what had just been designated the new city of Milton Keynes. It would be another ten years until the magnificent shopping centre opened, so Howard Hill had to order his college books from the local shop: titles like *The A to Z of Plumbing* and *Careers in Construction*. Hardly the stuff to turn a girl's head, but my mum says she fell for him straight away. By the time he asked her to lunch it was a done deal.

On the way back to the bookshop, Howard nipped into a

photo booth. He tried to cajole Maggie to go inside the booth with him but she thought this too forward. She did, however, accept one of the photographs with his telephone number and address scrawled on the back, and gave him her own number on a bookmark.

She still has the photo and is clutching it now, gazing out of watery eyes at the likeness of her husband thirty-eight years ago. Did he keep the bookmark? Somehow, I doubt it.

I walk up behind my mother and place a protective arm around her shoulders. She sinks into me as though melting. I am surprised when, instead of becoming more intense, her tears subside quickly. She still clings to me though, until my back is stiff from bending.

After a while I stand up straight and push her hair back from her face. She has continued to have it expensively dyed the copper-red of her youth, with expertly placed lowlights and highlights. It suits her. One day soon I'll remember to tell her.

'Cup of tea?' I say, and see, with a degree of discomfort, that she visibly relaxes. No reprimand from Stella this time. Is that really what she thinks? Is that what she expects from me?

She nods in agreement to the tea and begins to gather up the photographs, returning them to their black leather box. All except the passport photo; this she brings over to the sink where I'm washing out a cup.

'He was so handsome, wasn't he, back then?' she says softly, holding out the picture like a talisman.

I put the cup down on the granite worktop with a bang, harder than expected, making both of us jump. My fingers are clenched around the handle so tightly I can feel my nails digging into my palm. I should have seen that coming. She never passes up an opportunity to go on at me about my dad. Why don't I go and see him? Why did I take what happened so personally? Questions that I couldn't have made it plainer I have no intention of answering. Ever. Now she'll make a scene, more tears and recriminations.

Slowly, I uncurl my hand and walk across the kitchen to the fridge. My mother watches me carefully. I can feel her eyes boring into the back of my head, feel the weight of all the words she wants to say.

'Skimmed or semi?' I ask, turning to show her the choice of milk.

She slips the photograph into the pocket of her dressing gown and leaves the kitchen without another word. I stare at the space she leaves behind for a long time after she's gone.

***

The next shock of the day comes at eleven o'clock. I've just ended a particularly irksome phone call from a disgruntled tenant when my mobile rings in my bag under the desk. Thinking it might be Lipsy, I grab it and race out to the back of the building – personal calls are frowned upon even by ultra-lenient Paul. I'm still panting as I answer the phone.

'Can I speak to Miss Stella Hill, please?'

'Speaking.'

'This is Graham Canter from the Fire Investigations Office. We have a result in the investigation into your house fire. That is, we know what caused it.'

The voice is official and nasal. I fight to get my breath back and try to focus on what he is saying. The only words that register are "fire" and "caused".

'Was it arson?' I gasp.

'Was it… no, it wasn't arson, Miss Hill. Why would you think that?' He sounds worried all of a sudden. 'The police gave us no indication of suspicious circumstances …'

'No reason, just wondered,' I say quickly.

Of course it wasn't arson, I just have this uneasy feeling in my belly, and a strong conviction that someone must be to blame. A bad thing happens and it's somebody's fault. That's how it works, right?

'So? What was it then?' I force myself to ask.

58

'Your washing machine!' he announces triumphantly.

There is a long pause.

'My washing machine set fire to my house?' I say, incredulously. Visions invade my mind of the machine coming to life and dousing the kitchen in petrol, water hoses waving around menacingly, the round glass door a sinister moon-face.

'Indirectly, yes. It took us a while to figure it out, this fault is very rare. But we persevered, took apart every appliance, analysed every possible source of ignition. You wouldn't believe what you can deduce, even when something is terrifically damaged.'

He pauses as if waiting for praise or recognition. None is forthcoming so he carries on.

'A rare fault, as I said, seen in machines which are old and haven't been regularly serviced.'

'But …' I stammer, 'but, I – I didn't even have the washing machine on. I'd just got up, for God's sake!'

'The machine doesn't need to be going at the time. It was plugged in and left switched on. Something malfunctions, sparks fly, and the rest, as they say, is history.'

His voice recedes as the world starts to darken. I lean all my weight against the skip behind me and slide down it until I am sitting awkwardly on the ground. A cat, skinny and mangy, sleeks past me and picks at the remains of a kebab still in its wrapper. I watch it through flat eyes. The words echo and crash around my head.

Old machines. Not regularly serviced. Plugged in and left on. But I did this all the time, no one had ever told me not to, told me to unplug every appliance the minute I'd finished using it. And who knew they had to get their washing machine serviced? It breaks down you get it fixed. That was how we did it when I was growing up.

This is clearly no excuse, however. Reading between the lines, I know exactly what the jobsworth fire investigator is trying to tell me.

'Hello. Hello? Are you still there, Miss Hill?'

I drop the phone amidst the rubbish and put my head into my hands. He is trying to tell me that all of this is my fault and my fault alone. And the worst of it? I know it's true. I have burned down my own house through ignorance and neglect.

* * *

I stay late at the office again, waiting for my second date with Joshua. He called a little while ago to tell me that we're going to an upmarket restaurant recently opened by some friends of his.

I ponder his use of the word "upmarket". Does it mean he thinks my usual eateries are downmarket? Has he observed me bringing in my shopping bags (Happy Shopper and Lidl) and compared them unfavourably to his own Waitrose habit? Am I properly dressed for a meeting with high-flying restaurant-owning friends? Or should I race up to the shops again and buy another outfit, something more *upmarket*? Maybe just another pair of shoes?

After much agonising, I decide against it. There isn't much left of the sub Paul gave me and it's two more weeks until payday. Although I start my new job at Café Crème this Thursday – which I am really excited about – I'm planning to use my wages from there to buy something nice for Lipsy. Besides, I really can't summon up the energy to go shopping again. All those lovely things I can't afford – it's just too depressing.

I undo the top two buttons of my blouse instead and twist my hair up into a pleat, securing it with a purple butterfly clip I find in Susan's drawer. Lipstick and lashes follow. My reflection in the mirrored panels behind the displays isn't all that reassuring but it will have to do. What do I care, anyway? It's not as if I'm that interested in Joshua. But while I'm waiting for Mr Right I might as well let Mr Probably-Isn't buy me dinner occasionally.

Needing a distraction, I take out my list. Over the past week, it has become something of an obsession. The act of writing down on paper that which I most want has a magical feel, as though I can conjure items into existence with the power of my desire alone. I desperately need to believe that one day I will own stuff again.

Sometimes lately I feel weightless. It's as if I need possessions to give me substance. When I think about the few scant belongings I have left (capsule wardrobe, some teenage memorabilia, a seven-year-old Peugeot slightly the worse for wear), it makes me want to weep. I feel like a vagrant, homeless and possessionless in a world where everyone is judged by the amount of stuff they own.

Often it will be something small I'll miss, something triggered by a memory and followed by an achingly empty feeling in my stomach. Like the statue of the Eiffel Tower I brought home from a school trip when I was eleven: six inches tall and made of plastic; worthless and irreplaceable. Or the note on the fridge that had been there for over a year: Lipsy's careless scrawl, "Broke glass, sorry mum, love you." Those rare words – real written evidence that once my daughter felt that way about me. Thank God the photos did survive. No matter what Paul says, I *would* have rescued those from the fire ahead of my kitchenalia if I'd had the choice. I'm sure I would.

Unable to concentrate on the mountain of filing in front of me, I sit and stare out of the window, one hand on the stack of papers, the other on my list. Outside people are heading back to their cars, jackets flung over shoulders, arms full of shopping. I picture them arriving back at their homes, shrugging off shoes and flopping onto sofas with cups of tea or bottles of beer, and I have to fight back a fierce stab of envy.

* * *

At seven o'clock on the dot, Joshua pulls up outside Smart Homes in his super-sparkling Mazda. I leave the filing in a heap and lock the door behind me. It is a glorious evening, the kind Milton Keynes does really well. A low sun glints off the mirrored buildings and the long road down to the railway station is lined with trees and dotted with smiley people.

And what better way to enjoy it than from inside a sports car with the top down, speeding along dual carriageways, past lakes and parks. I'm glad I put my hair up (it would soon be a bird's nest otherwise), but I clocked Joshua's disappointment when he saw that I was wearing the same outfit as last week. Well, tough luck, Buster. I'm not a specimen for you to show off to your high-and-mighty friends.

This turns out to be an unfair assessment. His friends are warm and welcoming and completely unpretentious, a couple so obviously meant to be together it makes my heart hurt. Bob explains that he is doubling up as head chef for the night and leaves us with Charlotte, who carefully takes us through the menu. I watch her eyes as she talks, and wonder when was the last time I felt so enthusiastic about food.

While we wait for the wine to arrive I tell Joshua about the call from the fire investigator. He listens carefully and sympathetically and then makes me wish I hadn't told him at all.

'Stella, darling, you mustn't be so hard on yourself,' he says. 'Anyone could have made that mistake.' This may sound reassuring, but all it does is confirm that it was my fault, my mistake.

'Don't you leave your washing machine switched on when you're not using it?' I ask him.

'Of course not,' he laughs.

Why is it funny?

He sees my face and adds quickly, 'But that's because I do all my washing on a Sunday when I happen to be at home all day.'

'You clean your car then as well, don't you? And on a

Wednesday, if I'm not mistaken.' I am trying for a dig but he takes it as a compliment.

'You watch me a lot, huh?' He smiles, showing me lots of perfect teeth.

I shake my head indignantly but his attention has already wavered. Actually, I did watch him a lot, which is why his comment annoys me. I always made fun of his little obsessions, to Bonnie and Lipsy and to anyone else who was interested, but I found them reassuring. Like the way he always parks his car just so, never at an angle or haphazardly abandoned in the street (like me). And the way he closes his front door and then goes back three times to check it. I've seen him do this and it makes me smile – not always kindly, which seems a bit mean with hindsight.

But I didn't watch him because I fancied him, as he seems to be implying now. I guess I just didn't have a lot else to do – and yes, I know how sad that sounds.

I watch him again as he studies the wine list; we have ordered wine already but he clearly isn't entirely satisfied with his choice. I notice the way his hair grows straight back from his forehead and how it shows off his hairline, which is receding slightly. I like that in a man; I think it gives the face more definition. I went out with a guy once who had the lowest hairline you've ever seen; only an inch above his eyebrows, I swear. That relationship didn't last very long.

'I think we'll have a bottle of the Turning Leaf instead,' Joshua tells me. 'It will go better with the chicken.'

'Wouldn't it be a bit rude to change our order now?'

'No, don't be silly. Bob and Charlotte won't mind.'

He's probably right; they are possibly the most accommodating people I've ever met. But still, it seems a shame to abuse that. I keep my mouth shut; they are his friends, not mine.

Joshua tells a passing waiter about his change of mind then turns his attention back to me. He studies my face for five, ten, twenty seconds without even blinking. (Am I as interesting as the wine list?) His almond-shaped eyes make tiny little movements under immaculate eyebrows. I start to feel self-conscious, raise my hand to my face and say, 'What?'

He flashes me a smile and reaches across the table to take hold of my other hand. I look at it lying limply in his and notice that I've neglected my nails recently. They are uneven and chipped, a nasty sight. Joshua's perfectly manicured hand makes me want to curl my own up into a fist.

'Stella.' He squeezes to get my attention. I look up. 'I hope you don't mind me saying this but after what you told me I think I should speak out. Actually, I feel somewhat anxious. I don't want you to get upset.'

I'm surprised. I can't imagine what he thinks he could say to upset me. Plus, he neither looks nor sounds anxious. On the contrary, he is glowing, giving off a shiny heat like a panther I saw once at Whipsnade Zoo.

I smile at the image and have a feeling that Joshua would like being compared to a panther: sleek hair and muscular body, ready to pounce. Not that he's shown any signs of pouncing. He does seem more attentive than on our last date, though. Almost affectionate. I try to imagine us locked together, naked, in a passionate twist.

It makes me wish I still had my gym membership.

Joshua, taking my silent smile as consent, carries on.

'You probably don't know this, but I had thought about asking you out on a date before. I'd noticed you didn't have a boyfriend,' (I wince at this) 'and thought you were quite attractive. But the thing that stopped me, Stella, was, well, you do seem very disorganised.'

He practically spells the word out in syllables to emphasize it. I stare at him, open-mouthed. This is news to me.

'But now that this has happened, now that such an awful thing has happened to you, you're probably desperate to change. To get back some control in your life.' He squeezes my hand again, which has become rigid in his. 'And I would really like to help you, Stella. With a bit of planning and organisation, most problems can be avoided. If you're on top of things.

'Now, I,' he says, stretching his spine and flexing his well-developed neck, 'I have a system for almost everything: shopping, ironing, cleaning, maintenance, washing.'

These last two are thrown pointedly in my direction and they hit their target well.

I have two conflicting reactions to Joshua's damning assessment of my housekeeping abilities. Part of me is stung. Part of me, however, is strangely touched.

He wants to help me, to take me under his wing – his muscular, designer-clad wing – and nurse me back to being a fully functioning adult. An organised adult. Which is quite sweet in a way. I sit back and weigh him up. He's listing more of his personal systems now. He really is terrifyingly organised. I watch his mouth move around the words without actually listening to them, noticing how pink and well-defined his lips are.

Suddenly I realise that I don't find him remotely attractive. And the realisation makes me sad. It would be so easy if I did – so convenient, what with him living next door and all. But it doesn't matter how hard I try to convince myself, he just isn't my type. Still, there's nothing wrong with letting him have a stab at sorting my life out for me – he may well succeed where others have failed. He asks me a question. Something about a shopping budget. I nod sagely and smile in affirmation.

'Yes,' I tell him. 'Yes, whatever you say.'

Chapter 7

Lipsy

Thursday 14th June

I am having the week from hell. The woman formerly known as my mother is officially trying to ruin my life.

As if it's not enough that she's stopped me seeing Rob, grounded me, burnt down our house and everything in it, and left me destitute and desolate, now she's gone and got herself a part-time job in Café Crème – which she knows is where I go to meet Rosie, and now I will never have any peace, never ever ever.

It's not fair. It's not normal! Mothers are supposed to be married (preferably to your father) and have normal jobs in offices or boutiques. In extreme cases they can work in a high-street shop, but only one you never go into, and only if it's useful for a discount, say on computers or games. On no account can they work in any place their children or their children's friends visit. Everyone knows this. It causes extreme psychological problems according to Rosie, whose mum doesn't work at all because she has a husband who earns loads of dosh.

She didn't even tell me. I find out like this: I go into town to meet Rosie, figuring mum won't know I'm breaking my curfew because she's probably out somewhere with Bonnie or that bloke from next door. We meet by the bus station and walk up to Café Crème, pooling our change to see if we can afford an iced chocolate each. Rosie goes to get a table, our usual table by the window where we can watch everyone going past, and I go up to the counter.

I get my tray, I get my drinks, I go to pay – and there she is. My mother. Wearing one of those ridiculous yellow shirts they all wear, tied around her middle and showing off her belly – which is not a pretty sight – and laughing and smiling and waving at Rosie. As if this is a normal everyday thing. She didn't even – and I can't believe this – give me my drinks for free!

Lipsy stopped writing and threw her pen across the room. She was panting slightly, the memory, only an hour old, fresh and vividly painful. Why was her life turning so complicated? Just when she'd got herself a great boyfriend, a small group of admiring friends at school, an image, a lifestyle that fitted how she saw herself perfectly, why did it all have to start going wrong now?

At least Rob seemed to be hanging on, waiting for this ridiculous situation with her mother to sort itself out. But how long would he wait? She knew that he liked it when they were *together*, and most of her friends believed that if you weren't *doing it* with a bloke he'd dump you pretty quick. Suddenly the age difference seemed bigger, more important. He could go out when he liked, where he liked, while she, under the clutches of an overprotective mum, was grounded like a child. A child who couldn't *get with it*.

Lipsy wondered whether her code words would fool anyone, least of all her mother.

* * *

Stella

Tonight is my second shift at Café Crème. I'm doing Thursdays and Fridays, half five till nine, and Sundays, eleven till five. It takes up a lot of my free time, but what else would I be doing with it? Going rollerblading around Willen Lake? I hardly think so. That's more Paul's style than mine. All I have on my radar for the near future is decorating and more decorating, and without this job there will be no paint, so I'll just have to make the best of it.

So far I've managed to piss off one person by taking the job – and as that person is my daughter this is not a great start. I honestly thought she'd be pleased. I'm earning the money for her, for goodness sake, to buy her all that stuff she's so obsessed with. How was I to know that this exact coffee shop was her special place to hang out with her friend Rosie? Who is, it should be said, a little too grown-up for her age. She was wearing bras before she was out of nappies, that one.

I told Lipsy what I told my mother, and Joshua, and Bonnie – and everyone else who tried to give me their opinion on my latest course of action. This is my life, my problem, and it's up to me to sort it out. And this is the way I'm choosing. So there.

Paul comes in to see me around half eight. He's been showing a flat in the city centre, he says, but I know he's just come in to give me moral support. In fact, he's the only person who hasn't been down on my decision to get a second job, even going so far as to let me finish work half an hour early on Thursdays and Fridays. And he's given me a pay rise, bless him. Could he be any more thoughtful?

When it's his turn to be served (he lets two women go ahead of him so he can wait for me), I say, in my best waitress voice, 'And what can I get for you, Sir?'

'Well, now, let's see …' Paul begins to read the menu on the wall behind my head. 'I might go for the Mocha Frappuccino – what exactly would that be?'

'Erm, it's a chocolaty icy coffee thing.' But I haven't been shown how to make one yet. 'They're not very nice,' I whisper. 'Why not try our special, Sir?' I say loudly. 'The Cinnamon-Spiced Toffee Latte.'

Paul grins and nods, and I set about working the huge metal coffee machine and spooning spice mix into a tall glass. When it's done it doesn't look as much like the picture as I'd have liked, but Paul seems impressed. Until I tell him the price.

'How much? I could buy dinner for two for that,' he complains as he grudgingly hands over the cash.

I shush him and wave him off.

He carries his drink to a quiet corner and I wait a few seconds then announce to Gina that I'm going to do some clearing up while it's quiet. We close in half an hour, and I'm thinking I might see if Paul fancies getting something to eat; all this hard work makes me hungry.

'Speaking of dinner,' I say as I waft my cloth across the table next to his, 'are you busy later?'

'Are you asking me out on a date, Waitress?'

I stop my wafting and turn to look at him properly. He has that look in his eyes, the kind-of-naughty one I haven't seen for a while. I decide I like seeing it there very much, so I play along. 'Why, yes. I think I might be,' I say, coquettishly.

'Well, if we're going on a date I really should get to know you a bit better. Would you like to sit down?'

Looking around quickly, I spot Gina staring at her nails, totally bored, and our boss is nowhere to be seen. Coast clear. I perch on the edge of a chair, pulling in my tummy so it doesn't overhang. Blast these silly tie-waist shirts.

'So, Mister,' I say, 'what would you like to know?'

Leaning across the small wooden table, Paul rests his hands over mine and asks me, with a completely straight face, 'Would you like to get married someday?'

I jump back so fast I nearly fall off my chair. Suddenly our harmless, silly flirting doesn't seem so harmless at all. Paul is laughing but he looks a bit uncomfortable. I try to smooth over my extreme reaction with a joke of my own.

'Be careful, Mister. I might say yes,' I answer in a sing-song voice.

It doesn't work. I don't know why exactly, but the light,

fun mood of moments ago has been replaced by a heavy, awkward silence. Paul is looking at me strangely, his blue eyes unreadable. Deep and unreadable, just like they were in school when I'd dream night after night that he would ask me that very question one day – but obviously not in jest. What would have happened if I hadn't met John Dean when I did? If I'd waited around just a little bit longer, given our friendship a chance to become something more? Would he have noticed me then as more than just Stella From School? All these years he's watched out for me like I'm his little sister or something, and I bet it has never occurred to him that we could have been so much more. Could still be so much more…

'I'd better go and help finish up,' I say, standing. I can hear Gina dismantling the coffee machines ready for cleaning. My cue to move my arse.

Paul nods. Dinner, it seems, is forgotten. I can't describe the odd feeling in my stomach right now.

Just then I notice a man out of the corner of my eye. He is lurking outside the door of Café Crème, wearing a tatty parka (even though it's June) and carrying a traveller's rucksack.

My first thought: We're closed, mate, go away.

My second thought: Oh my God. It's my brother.

Catching my eye through the window, Billy waves energetically and then pushes open the door.

'Sorry, we're closed,' Gina calls from behind the counter.

'It's OK, he's with me,' I tell her. She looks from me to Paul to Billy and back again, shakes her head and returns to her cleaning.

I intercept my brother as he claps Paul on the back and drops his backpack to the floor.

'Long time no see, sis,' he says, all smiles, like butter wouldn't melt in his mouth. I'd really like to shove a load in there and test that theory out.

'What the bloody hell are you doing here?'

I'm fuming. Yes, this is my brother, but the last time I saw him he had two hundred quid of mine in his grubby paws – a loan for his rent, supposedly, to be paid back in less than a month.

That was eighteen months ago.

Here he is now, turning up like an odd sock you can never find a match for but can't bear to throw away. He stands awkwardly, hands shoved deep into his pockets, shoulders hunched. Billy is taller than me but we look about the same height due to his terrible posture; not a manifestation of poor self-esteem, more a sign of laziness. He slumped suddenly at thirteen and has never bothered stretching out his spine since, and no amount of nagging from our mother, or knees in the back from our father, made the slightest difference.

Little Billy Bobby-Socks was what we all called him when he was born, due to his comically over-large feet and the ridiculous bright orange socks my grandmother knitted him. He was the most beautiful baby I'd ever seen (I hadn't seen many), with big blue eyes and a red, petal-shaped mouth that emitted ear-splitting wails and cute gurgles in equal measure. I was seven, and had all but despaired of having a sibling to play with.

So the boy had quite a lot to put up with for the first few years of his life as I dressed him in dolls' clothes and made him the guest of honour at imaginary tea parties. When I was ten and began to experiment with make-up, guess who I tried out my favourite colours on?

I suppose, in retrospect, it's surprising he turned out as well as he did. But the point I am trying to make is this: with all that gentle, feminine influence so early on, how did he manage to become such a rough and ready, sleeping-under-the-stars type of bloke? Were all those hours spent putting my mum's old tights on his head and pretending it was long hair for nothing?

Anyway, it's not just the money he took, although that has rankled occasionally over the last year and a half while I've struggled to support my daughter, and bail out our mum. It's not just that I didn't know where he was, either. I figured he'd turn up sooner or later.

No, the main reason I am well and truly pissed off with my brother is that he ran away and left us at a really bad time. A really, really bad time. Just after our father had been sentenced to three years in prison. We were all struggling to come to terms with that, not to mention the newly impoverished state the cost of the trial – and the fine – had left my mother in.

But I don't want to talk about that.

So, anyway, Billy, he just walks away without telling a soul, two hundred pounds of his sister's hard-earned cash in his back pocket, the rest of his belongings in his backpack. Like some kind of hobo. Mum got a postcard from Cornwall two months later letting her know he was OK. By that time none of us cared very much.

And here he sits now, looking like he's been living in a tree for the past year, dirty and dishevelled and completely unbothered by my not-so-chuffed reaction.

'Stel's a bit grumpy today, isn't she,' he says to Paul, who has the decency to look embarrassed. For the second time in ten minutes, bless him.

'I don't believe you.' I shake my head, at a loss for anything more expressive to say. 'I really don't believe you.'

I spend the next fifteen minutes furiously clearing tables, assiduously ignoring Billy's attempts to talk to me. I can hear him telling Paul all about his "adventures", as he calls them, and I pick up the odd word or place name here and there. I'm not interested. Tony comes out and dangles the keys ready to lock up, and I gesture to Paul that it's time to go.

'I'm taking your brother back to mine,' he says. 'He can stay with me for a few days, it's no bother.'

I lay a hand on his arm. 'You don't have to do that, Paul.'

'I know. But I want to help. Bye, Stella.'

As they leave, Billy a lanky streak of mud beside Paul in his sharp suit, I feel an odd pulling at my heart. But the weird thing is, I have absolutely no idea which of the two is doing it.

Chapter 8

Stella

I may have mentioned it before once or twice, but I hate my mother's lodger. He's kind of omnipresent – a leech in our lives – although my mother can't see this, and even Lipsy, normally full of scorn for anyone over the age of twenty, seems to be warming to him. So I'm on my own here, waging my own battle. And, unfortunately, so far I'm losing quite badly.

There is something not right about him, mark my words, and the fact that he never pays his rent on time, eats my mother's food instead of buying his own, and has an opinion on just about everything is neither here nor there.

What's weird is the way he has of appearing whenever there is trouble to be stirred up. Like now, for example. Mum and I are arguing about the same thing we always argue about: her spending. My patience is wearing so thin it is virtually anorexic, and there she is ordering a new bathroom suite because the existing one is "a bit dated". Is this woman for real?

'There is absolutely no way you are having a new bathroom and that's final,' I tell her in my sternest, don't-mess-with-me voice, which used to work wonders on Lipsy until she was about nine-years-old.

We are in her living room, accompanied by a seemingly endless rerun of *Top Gear* on the TV. This should have indicated the presence of Alistair but I am too outraged to notice.

'But I've already ordered it, Stella. It's too late to cancel now.' This is my mother's argument. See what I'm up against here?

'What were you doing ordering it in the first place? You don't have any money, Mum. How are you going to pay for it?'

She stares at me blankly, playing with a piece of her hair, twirling it round and round her finger. She does this whenever she's anxious. There'll be no other outward signs of distress, just this incessant twirling and fiddling until finally her hair becomes tangled up like a bird's nest. And who will have to help her get the knots out? You guessed it.

'Don't be angry, Stella,' she pleads. 'I thought it would be nice, for Lipsy and you, as you're both staying here now. I thought you'd be pleased.'

I look at her in astonishment. Is the woman completely demented?

'You thought I would be pleased? You thought that even though my own house is a burnt-out wreck, even though I have virtually no belongings and I'm working two jobs to get the money to do up the aforementioned wreck, you thought I would be happy to see my mother run up even more debt on her credit cards? Because that's how you're planning to pay for it, isn't it? On your maxed-out credit cards?'

It is at that precise moment that a pointed cough at my back tells me Alistair is in the room and about to have his say.

'You really oughtn't talk to your mother that way, Stella.'

Just the sound of his voice sets my teeth on edge. I don't turn around, instead I carry on speaking as though he's not there. My mother looks like a rabbit caught in headlights. It is tearing at my heart having to do this to her but I have to make her see sense.

'This has to stop, Mum,' I say, very quietly. 'You and I both know you can't go on like this. I can't afford to bail you out again and I'm worried about you. We need to talk about this properly. And privately,' I add, with a tilt of my head towards Alistair.

My mother nods slowly, dropping her hand from her hair to rest on her stomach. I relax, believing we are on the brink of a breakthrough, and I start to imagine a proper, grown-up conversation where we finally come up with a coping strategy.

Then Alistair speaks again.

'Why don't you just give it a rest, eh, Stella? Some of us are trying to relax here and that's a bit difficult when you're shrieking like a banshee. You need to chill out a bit, yeah?' He grabs the TV remote and turns the volume up to a deafening level, all the time looking at me with a challenging smirk.

Frozen in place, I can't believe my ears. Has this free-loading little git just told me to shut up? In my own mother's house?

Yes, he has. And it looks like he's also going to get away with it. At least, as far as my mother's concerned. I know she hates confrontation – don't we all? – but surely she can't stand back and let that go unchallenged?

'Are you going to let your *lodger* speak to your own *daughter* like that?' I glare at my mother who won't meet my eyes.

Alistair carries on watching TV, laughing uproariously at some sycophantic joke. I hate *Top Gear* almost as much as I hate him.

I walk to the door and turn back to face them both, close to tears but not going to let either of them see that. Shaking my hair back from my face I say to my mother, 'I refuse to live under the same roof as that man. You have one week. Either he goes or I go. And as for your new bathroom – do whatever you like.'

* * *

'Where do you want this to go, Stella?'

I look from Paul to the box and back again. The fact is, I've got no idea where I want anything to go – but then, as I have so little I don't suppose I'll have to make too many of these decisions just yet. The box Paul is holding contains some of the basic kitchen equipment I've begged and borrowed over the past week (I'm drawing the line at stealing for now), so I ask him to stick it in the kitchen.

'Hey,' he calls, 'it's looking so much better in here.'

He is lying, but I appreciate the gesture. The old kitchen cupboards have been stripped out and dumped, and I've washed down the walls and bashed off the old tiles and ripped up the floor. So basically it looks like an empty room after a fire, but I guess that's a few steps up from a bomb site.

It is exactly a week since I delivered my ultimatum to my mother, and if there's one thing every parent knows it's to always carry out what you threaten to do. I'm sure Lipsy would be even further off the rails if I hadn't been firm with her, and now my mother is suffering the same treatment. Oh, she cried a little and begged me not to go, but I stood firm. Even when my daughter announced she wasn't coming with me. That was a tough moment, I can tell you. But then I figured that Lipsy might be better off staying behind for a while, at least until her own home had a functioning kitchen and bathroom. I can rough it. I have no choice. I know I shouldn't expect Lipsy to rough it with me. Although, it would have been nice.

Anyway, as soon as she sees what a great job I'm doing here she'll be dying to come back. That's the plan. Paul is being a rock as usual, and having the use of Smart Homes' handyman, Ray, is a real bonus. He's coming tomorrow to sort out the bathroom, which is a bit of a priority. Being able to wash always helps, I find.

'Paul.' I grab his arm as he walks past with the last of the boxes.

'Huh?'

'Just wanted to say thanks.'

'Go on then.'

'What?'

'Say thanks.'

I laugh and nudge him in the ribs, knowing he can't defend himself. 'Thank you very much, O great one,' I say, bowing a little and letting go of his arm. He grins and carries on by me. 'Seriously, Paul, I am grateful. I couldn't have got through this week without you. And letting me use Ray to do some of the work, well, I don't know what to say. You've saved my life.'

'You don't have to say anything.' Paul comes back out of the kitchen and sits on one of the garden chairs I "borrowed" from my mother's garage. 'And I haven't saved your life. Yet,' he adds, fixing my eyes with his. 'Although I may do, one day.'

I don't know quite what's been happening between us lately. Actually, when I say 'between us' I really mean 'to me', because Paul is just being Paul, joking around and play-flirting, same as he always has. I know it doesn't mean anything. It's just that lately I've started to wish it did.

He's my oldest friend, and it's no secret that I had a crippling crush on him as a kid. I thought I was over all that long ago. Maybe, maybe not. Maybe it's the way he's so attentive and caring, the way that whenever I talk he makes me feel as though I'm the only person in the room. He does that with everyone, of course, not just me. He's that kind of guy. Which makes it even harder to ignore the feelings that are pushing themselves up mercilessly from a place I thought I'd buried them years ago.

I look at him now, leaning back into the deckchair, flexing his shoulders a little but looking perfectly relaxed and at home. He's wearing jogging pants and an old washed-out T-shirt but still looks like he's just walked off the pages of a catalogue. We've spent a lot of time together this week, sorting out stuff for the house, sharing a pizza after work a few times, and I don't think I'd be exaggerating to say we're getting closer. Closer than just-good-friends.

No, I don't think I'd be exaggerating at all.

A few nights ago, Joshua called to ask me out again and I agreed to meet him for a drink, just for something to do, really. But the strangest thing happened. All I could think about all evening was Paul. Paul, my boss. Paul, my best friend. He filled my head so much that I called Joshua "Paul" twice.

Now, I think I know what is going on here, and it isn't necessarily that I've lost my marbles. Since the fire, I've been feeling rootless and cast adrift in a possession-free world. I go on a couple of dates with Joshua and, even though he *so* isn't the one for me, I begin to imagine what it would be like to be with a man again. Really *with* a man. What it would be like to be *in love*. Maybe deep down I feel that I kind of need a little bit of rescuing…

Impressed by my amateur psychology? Well, don't be. It's Bonnie's theory, not mine. But it struck a chord with me, and I was intrigued to think that all this could be going on without my knowledge. I have hidden depths. I've always suspected as much.

Anyway, once these secret desires were reawakened (Bonnie again), they were free to attach themselves to their *true* target.

And that target is by my side right now, unaware and unknowing.

I lower myself into a matching deckchair, aware for the first time today that I'm not wearing any make-up and haven't washed my hair for two days. Surreptitiously, I undo the top button on my shirt as though this will make me suddenly irresistible. Ha!

Paul moves his chair nearer to mine and all my nerves tingle. There is a look on his face that I have seen somewhere before, in another lifetime.

Might Paul feel the same way about me as I think I've started to feel about him?

The house is silent except for the beating of my heart. I watch his face as he considers me for a moment and then begins to speak.

'Stella. There's something I want to talk to you about.'

This is it. Declarations of undying love surely to follow. I hope so, I really, really hope so. If only because it will spare me the ordeal of having to be the one to bring it up. (Very romantic, Stella!)

'Yes?' I say breathily. 'What is it?'

'I want to talk to you about Billy.'

'Billy?'

'Yes, Billy. You know – your brother.'

'I know who he is.' Inwardly I seethe. Bloody Billy getting in the way again: perfect timing as usual. 'What about him?'

Paul leans forward and takes my hand. Oh-ho, maybe it's not so bad after all.

'He's sorry about the way he left, you know. He feels dreadful about it. And he'd like a chance to make it up to you.' Paul smiles and my heart jumps. How could I have worked right next to the man for all this time and ignored how gorgeous his smile is?

'OK,' is all I can think of to say.

Paul gets off his garden chair and comes to kneel by my feet, the traditional position of proposal. Suddenly I can see it all: the wedding, my dress, Paul looking devastating in his morning suit, all our family and friends smiling indulgently, paper confetti in rainbow hues...

'Stella?' And back to reality.

'Stella, I know you've been through a really bad time lately, and I really admire how you've been coping. But the thing is...'

I drift off again as Paul carries on talking, his face sincere and thoughtful. He's saying something about Billy and my father but I'm not listening. I'm just looking at him. Looking at his mouth. His full, strong, mobile mouth. And before I even know what I'm about to do I lean forward and lay my lips against it.

For a beautiful ten seconds, our lips blend in perfect harmony. My head tilts to one side to get a better angle and my hand begins to creep up his arm, feeling the taut muscles under the thin fabric.

Then, as suddenly as it began, it is over, and Paul is looking at me with an expression on his face that can only be described as horror.

'Stella! What are you doing?'

Oh my God. I've made a terrible mistake.

I try to think of a way to pass it off as a joke but my mind is still reeling, partly from residual pleasure and partly from the shock that I could have got it so wrong.

Forcing myself to laugh, I sit back and say, 'God, what was I thinking? For a moment there I thought you were Brad Pitt. Must be the shock of being back in this place.' It is weak, but it's the best I can do under the circumstances.

'Brad Pitt?' Paul repeats doubtfully. Great, now he is regarding me with something close to sympathy. That's the last thing I wanted.

I could tell him that confusing him with Brad Pitt would be impossible because Paul is better looking by far. I could tell him that I can't imagine not having him in my life now and that I want more than just his friendship – much, much more. But I can't find the words. Instead, I get up and head for the kitchen and the ever-reliable crutch of making tea.

Paul follows me and leans against the makeshift table, lowering his head to try and see my eyes. 'Was that what I think it was?' he asks me gently.

I nod and then shrug. There is no point trying to hide it. He can see through me completely, always has done.

'But I can see I got it wrong,' I tell him with a brave smile. 'Which is fine. Can we just drop it now?' Teabags go in mugs, milk sloshes over sides of mugs, kettle starts to boil frantically. I keep my face away from him, terrified I might cry and do even more damage.

Ever the sensitive one, Paul takes the hint and leaves me to it. I can hear him shuffling boxes around in the lounge while I finish making tea. By the time I join him I'm just about OK. Now, as long as he's not nice to me I'll be fine.

'Stella,' Paul says softly, taking the mugs out of my hands and standing them on the floor, 'I'm so sorry I reacted like that. I'm flattered, I really am.'

I try to brush it off again but he stops me with a finger on my mouth.

'You are a wonderful woman. Beautiful, intelligent, funny, sexy…' He pauses and I wonder if he's run out of nice things to say about me. Not that it matters. However wonderful he thinks I am, one thing's for certain: he doesn't want to play tongue-hockey with me.

'Paul, it's OK. I just, you know, got a bit crazy for a moment. Please, *please*, can we forget all about it now?'

He nods, still dreadfully serious. 'It's only that I'm not ready for a relationship,' he explains earnestly. 'With anyone. I love my life just as it is and I don't want it to change. My life is uncomplicated and that's just the way I like it.'

'Me too!' I lie, and we look at each other for a moment before bursting out laughing. 'Still friends?' I say lightly.

'Still friends,' Paul agrees. 'Always.'

'Always.'

But as I sip my disgusting tea I find myself wondering whether somehow my faux pas might have changed our friendship forever. Only time will tell.

Chapter 9

Lipsy

W*ednesday 27*[th] *June*

Today is not a good day.

When these diaries are published I think today may stand out as one of the worst days ever – worse even than the day I discovered that Will Young is gay. But first, I must report on other matters.

The situation with my mother has improved a lot, mainly because she's moved out of Grandma's and they've lifted my curfew. So I can see Rob as much as I want, which is great. It's been nearly a month since the fire though, and there's no sign of things getting back to normal anytime soon. I'm getting just a little bit sick of being stuck in this room with nothing to do. I know I should be going into school but as I'm not planning on taking any exams and I'm leaving soon anyway it seems like a waste of time.

I saw my dad yesterday, for the first time in ages. He's actually really cool, and he was great about me and Rob, not all hysterical like my mum. He tried to give me a lecture about contraception and stuff but I think he was too embarrassed. Bet my mother put him up to it, that would be so like her. Anyway, he gave me some money to buy myself some new clothes and promised to go and talk to mum about Rob. If she just gave Rob a chance she'd see he's great.

Rosie's getting on my nerves. She keeps wanting to go to Café Crème and laugh at my mum in her stupid uniform. I mean, yes, she looks daft but does Rosie have to go on and on about it? At least my mum is trying to get money and stuff, at least she cares. Rosie's mum doesn't care about anything except golf. And she's ugly, whereas my mum, although she's completely mental, is also fairly hot – according to the guys at school anyway. Maybe I should ask her what her secret is?

But I can't think about any of these things right now. I have to go to the bathroom any minute and check again. I'm five days late. Not good. Very, very bad. I told Rob we should have used something. I'm not stupid. But he said he'd pull out beforehand. He said that was safe. And he should know. And we've only done it a few times, and the third time he was pretty drunk. You can't get pregnant that easily, can you? Please God, don't let me be that unlucky.

Please, please, please ...

* * *

Paul

Paul let himself into his flat and stood with his back to the door, listening. Silence. That was good. That meant Billy was out and he had the place to himself. Not that he minded having Stella's brother staying with him – Billy was a good laugh (in small doses) and Paul was glad to be able to help out. But, still. It was nice to have a bit of 'personal space' as the guys at work would call it.

Paul thought about Stella while he checked the flat to make sure it really was empty. He hoped she wasn't dwelling on what had happened earlier – he'd gone to great lengths to reassure her that they could easily forget all about it and carry on as before. He pushed the memory of that kiss firmly out of his mind. It would have been so easy, so natural, to have just taken her in his arms and … No! She was a friend, a good friend, and he wasn't about to ruin that. What he'd told her was nothing more than the truth – he just didn't want to be in a relationship. With anyone. It was as simple as that.

He grabbed a beer from the fridge and pressed the button on the answerphone. Two messages: one from Nick cancelling their poker night, the other from Andrew bowing out of squash – some excuse about a sprained ankle. Funny how the sprained ankle coincided with Andrew getting a new girlfriend – the nubile Rachel that Paul had had to hear all about last weekend.

So much for friends, he thought, picking up the day's post, which was piled in an unruly heap on the worktop. Bills, more bills, a circular for double glazing. A postcard from his mate Dave, holidaying in Spain, lucky bugger. And a hand-written purple envelope with a big fat letter inside.

Paul looked at this with interest. Turning it over he noted there was no return address and that the envelope was thick and plush and distinctly feminine. He tore it open carefully, then tipped the contents out onto the coffee table. Five or six purple sheets opened up like a fan revealing large, looped handwriting in blue biro.

He dropped onto the sofa and started to read. While his beer went flat, Paul clutched the sheets of paper in shaking hands, reading and re-reading the words until they were etched indelibly into his brain.

Sharon. The sweet, unchallenging beautician from Bletchley. A woman he'd dated, and unintentionally hurt, more than nine years ago, now back in his life via a purple letter. And with a huge surprise up her sleeve.

He never even knew there had been a baby. A *pregnancy*, yes. And he'd tried, he really had tried, to be supportive in every way possible. Except for the one way that wasn't possible, not for him, as he knew he didn't love her and he knew he couldn't stay around forever, to give her what she needed and deserved.

'But I would have supported her,' he said to the empty room, 'and the baby, if I'd known that was what she wanted.' Feelings of guilt, long-buried, rose cruelly to the surface, and Paul felt his eyes blur, his legs grow heavy and weak.

'I didn't even know she wanted to keep it,' he whispered.

But keep it she had. Secretly, without his help or his knowledge, she'd decided to go ahead and have the baby, and never to tell its father it even existed. Until now. The letter didn't explain why. In fact, for such a long letter, it held few of the details that Paul so desperately wanted to know. The only detail he had, and the one he returned to again and again with a strange combination of elation and panic, was that out there somewhere, he, Paul Smart, confirmed bachelor and lover of all things single, had a beautiful eight-year-old daughter.

* * *

Stella

By Sunday morning I have recovered my equilibrium enough to put the whole Paul fiasco into perspective. In fact, I am even starting to believe my lie – that being back at the scene of my recent disaster, and with the prospect of staying here alone for the first time since the fire looming, I had taken leave of my senses and gone a little crazy. It could have been anyone; it happened to be Paul. It certainly didn't mean anything.

It didn't mean anything at all.

That said, I'm still planning to keep a low profile for a few days, which, as we work together, could prove tricky. I'll just have to keep my head down, that's all. Get stuck into work for once. Give Loretta the shock of her life.

I spend the morning washing down the walls in the lounge and the hallway. With music blaring from the portable stereo I "borrowed" from my mother's kitchen, and a cheerful breeze blowing through the house via the open front door, sweeping away the last of the horrid musty smell, I find I'm feeling almost happy.

When my hair gets in my eyes I grab one of the rags from the pile on the floor and tie it around my head, washerwoman style. When I have to kneel for a while to tackle the skirting boards I use more rags to make pads for my knees. And when a favourite song comes on the radio I turn the broom over and pretend it's a microphone, belting out the words at the top of my voice.

Unfortunately, this is how Paul finds me when he sticks his head around the front door just before lunchtime. So much for keeping a low profile.

'Stella!' He manages to suppress a smile but I can see his eyes flickering over my bizarre appearance. He probably thinks his rejection has sent me completely over the edge.

'Paul,' I reply nonchalantly. Oh, I've suffered worse embarrassments than this. The secret is to brazen it out, pretend you're not bothered. 'And what can I do for you?' I flip the broom back over and start to scrub the ceiling, accidentally flicking water all over him.

He retreats to the kitchen and calls out, 'Do you think you could leave that for ten minutes? I wanted to have a word with you.'

'Sure.'

I'm due a break anyway, so I join him in the kitchen, pleased to see he hasn't come empty-handed. As well as sandwiches and a bottle of coke, he's brought two fold-up chairs that he arranges on either side of the pasting table. Very cosy. We sit and I eat, watching him warily.

'So, what's this word you want to have?' I ask coolly. I hope it's not another sorry; I really would like to forget the whole thing. That's twice I've made a fool of myself over Paul Smart, and I'm certainly not going to do it again.

I needn't have worried. Paul's news has nothing to do with me – or us – but it leaves me reeling all the same.

'*You* have a daughter?' I say, too shocked to censure the emphasis out of my voice.

89

'Is that so hard to believe?' he snaps. I don't know why he's being so touchy – you have to admit it's a bit of a leap to go from bachelor-Paul to daddy-Paul in the space of twenty-four hours.

To calm him down I ask more appropriate questions: How old is she? Where do they live? What is this 'Sharon' person like? Paul looks up warily at this but I smile and make my eyes wide, as though I'm merely interested.

Of course I'm suspicious. Or maybe protective is a better word. (Jealous is certainly not a word I'd use.) After all, Paul is a successful man with his own business, a penthouse flat, all the trappings of a great catch. Fair game for an unscrupulous woman with a claim on his affections from years ago.

'So,' I say as casually as possible, 'why is she telling you about this now? After all this time?'

'I'm not sure. In her letter, she says that she wanted to go it alone at first, didn't want me to feel obligated. But she says that lately, Hannah has been asking about her daddy. And she didn't want to lie to her. She says she wants to know if I'm willing to have a relationship with Hannah before she tells her anything.'

I nod slowly. 'That sounds…' I want to say 'plausible' but stop myself just in time. 'Responsible,' I say instead.

'Yes, it does, doesn't it?'

'So do you?'

'Do I what?'

'Do you want to have a relationship with her? With Hannah?' I add, carefully. I remember Paul telling me in no uncertain terms only yesterday how happy he was with his life just the way it is, and how he wasn't ready for a relationship. With anyone. I'm guessing this isn't the kind he had in mind.

He looks so sad for a moment that I have to suppress the urge to put my arms around him. Two days ago that's exactly what I would have done, but now I can't. So much for my actions having no effect on our friendship.

'Yes,' he tells me earnestly. 'Yes, I want that very much.'

I'm not surprised. Paul isn't the kind of man to shy away from his responsibilities. It's what makes him so special. Nothing like Lipsy's dad, who wouldn't know responsibility if it jumped up and smacked him in the face.

'So what happens next?'

'I don't know. I've got her phone number, she put it in the letter. I guess I'll call her and arrange to go and see them.' There is a look of hope and excitement around his eyes that makes me a little worried.

'Just don't go building your hopes up, OK.'

'What do you mean?' he asks.

'Well,' I say slowly, 'it's been nine years since you've seen this woman. You don't know anything about her circumstances right now. You haven't heard from her for years and you've never even laid eyes on this Hannah. Just be careful, that's all.'

'Of what, exactly?' He isn't looking too happy now. Why do I have to be the one to burst his bubble? How naive can a person be?

'There is a chance,' I say, carefully, 'just a chance, that this child might not actually be, well, yours.'

Paul glares at me, horrified. 'You think Sharon might be making it up?'

'No, I'm just saying that there's a chance, that's all. And that you should keep an open mind.' I don't add, 'And ask for a paternity test'. I stop myself just in time.

'But what reason would she have for lying?'

'I don't know, Paul.' His naivety is starting to annoy me. For someone who doesn't want any kind of commitment, he certainly seems attached to the idea of having a daughter already.

Maybe some of my bitterness has seeped out without me noticing. Paul eyes me carefully and then shakes his head.

'This is about yesterday, isn't it? You're still pissed off with me and you're being a killjoy. I thought better of you, Stella. I really did. I thought you'd be happy for me.'

I protest my innocence but it's too late. Paul is getting up to leave and I know I've gone too far. How did it come to this? How did our rock-solid friendship get so shaky?

'I'm just trying to be a friend, that's all,' I call out to his departing back. 'I'm trying to be realistic.'

He leaves without answering and I sit for a long time looking at my streaky walls.

Realistic was the word I used to justify my warnings. But I know better than anyone there is a fine line between realism and pessimism. A very fine line indeed.

Chapter 10

Stella

I'm on the phone to Bonnie, trying to hide the fact that it's a personal call from the rest of the office while simultaneously keeping an eye out for Paul, who is unusually absent for a Monday morning. Bonnie has been quizzing me about Joshua – she feels responsible, she said, after setting me up with him. I tell her that Joshua is almost certainly a lost cause as a boyfriend, but is turning out to be a really good neighbour and friend. As well as a filing cabinet, he's also bought me my own body weight in cleaning materials and enough air freshener to fumigate a pig farm. He almost certainly has obsessive-compulsive disorder, but is this necessarily a bad thing in a mate when you have a house that needs serious organising and renovating?

I decide not to tell her about throwing myself at Paul, or the feelings I'm not-so-secretly harbouring for him. Bonnie doesn't understand the complicated machinations which usually make up a love life, especially mine. She keeps hers simple: nice, unchallenging bloke with a constant cash flow providing meals out and cosy nights in; rows restricted to which film to see or whose set of friends to invite over that weekend. That's not to say I'm criticising her lifestyle – envying it more like. But I know it wouldn't work for me, any more than mine would work for her. Perhaps that's why we get on so well: opposites attract and no competition.

She says goodbye with a promise to come over and wield a paintbrush very soon (that I'd like to see), and I replace the phone just as Loretta comes back from lunch smiling – smiling! – and carrying a box that would, in the hands of a normal person, be filled with cakes.

'What have you got there, Loretta?' calls Joe from his desk.

'Cakes,' Loretta announces, setting them down on her immaculate desk, 'and carrot cake for anyone who's on a diet.'

I wait for her to look pointedly in my direction but she doesn't.

Shaking my head in amazement, I turn my attention back to my growing mound of typing. Working Loretta out is beyond my capabilities, and not top of my list right now. My number one priority is getting my house into a habitable enough state for Lipsy to move back into. For some reason – naivety, blind hope – I had thought she would get fed up with being at my mother's, in her old bedroom filled with soft toys and kids' games, and slip back home one day, sulking and moaning but still irrevocably there. I imagined the first I'd know of it would be hearing her awful music pounding down the stairs, or going to the fridge to find it emptied of all food.

Of course, this would be a lot easier if I actually had a fridge.

After a few hours of typing – or possibly only minutes but time is dragging today – I notice that Paul is back in his cubbyhole. Picking up the cream cake I saved for him I manoeuvre my way around the filing cabinet arrangement and creep up behind him.

'Surprise,' I say softly, laying a hand on his shoulder – his muscular, very square, very toned shoulder – and trying not to be offended when he flinches and jumps to his feet.

'Oh,' he says, 'it's you.'

'Well, yes. It is me. And there's no need to look so pleased about it.'

'Sorry. You just made me jump.'

I perch on the corner of his desk as he sits back down and rests his fingers on the keyboard.

'Who else would it have been, anyway?' I ask. 'Who else would come in and grope their boss in the middle of the day?'

Thankfully I'm rewarded with a rueful smile. It seems a delicate truce has been restored. I vow not to blow it again.

'You wouldn't want to know,' he says, and I catch him as his eyes sweep the room in the direction of Loretta. Then I notice the biggest, creamiest cake of all on his desk.

'No!' I'm actually quite shocked. 'Not Loretta? Has she got the hots for you, Smart?' I laugh, going for amused but it comes out slightly hysterical.

What do I care if old bulldog face has taken a shine to the object of my affection? Until recently I'd have thought it hysterically funny – before I had my epiphany and realised the nature of my true feelings. At least, I *think* I would.

I decide I won't resent Loretta her little infatuation. If wanting to make Paul happy brings on cream cakes and smiles, who am I to complain? And Paul does seem in desperate need of cheering up today. I just hope it's not entirely my fault.

'Paul,' I say, deciding on the direct approach, 'are you still mad at me for what I said about Hannah?'

He jumps again, accidentally hitting a combination of keys that makes his screen go black. 'Crap!' he grumbles through gritted teeth, and I find myself apologising, although I'm not sure what for.

'Maybe I should leave you to it?' I try not to sound too dejected as I slide off his desk and smooth down my skirt.

'Stella, wait.' Paul catches my hand. His palm is warm and I long to hold it against my cheek. 'I know you only said what you said because you care. And I understand why you would be suspicious, you're only looking out for me. But,' he says, his eyes so innocent and sincere, 'I have no doubts at all that Sharon is telling the truth and Hannah is mine. And I really don't want to discuss it with you again. OK?'

I nod mutely. But it isn't OK at all.

***

I slip away from work early; with Loretta still in her strange good mood and Paul sulking in his hidey-hole. Back at the house, I start work straight away on my bathroom. I actually have one now – our odd-job man installed it this morning. Now all I need to do is put up new tiles, fit a shower and a shower curtain, paint, put up shelves and a cabinet and a mirror, and it'll be finished.

So, no problem then.

Except for one small, teeny-weeny hitch. I haven't got a clue what I'm doing.

There are women who are good at DIY and there are women who aren't. Of those who aren't, there are two distinct types: women like Bonnie who can afford to "get a man in" to do whatever job they need, and the type who can't afford it and are therefore reduced to visiting the library and pouring over centuries-old books on tiling or wallpapering, and then turning Do-It-Yourself into Destroy-It-Yourself. And you guessed it – I belong to the second type.

I do a quick mental recce of all the men I know in case there are any useful skills I can call upon.

Joshua isn't the hands-on type so he's out, although I imagine he'll be happy to help me clear up afterwards. Paul – best not to ask for any more favours from him right now. Bonnie's Marcus will be great when I can finally afford a new computer and need it setting up. But not, I think, tiling. Alistair – urghh, don't even go there!

Which just leaves my feckless brother, who I've avoided despite what Paul said about him wanting to make up with me. He certainly owes me a few favours, but if he has any skills I'm not sure what they are, and to be honest I'd rather ruin the bathroom myself than be beholden to him.

This is a tricky spot I find myself in, with no easy answers, no way to charm my way out of it, and a strong aversion to getting down and dirty with the dark side of decorating.

But fate does indeed work in mysterious ways.

I'm putting on my shoes ready for that trip to the library when there is a knock on the door. I open it to find, standing in front of me, large as life and ten times as handsome, John Dean.

Lipsy's father. The man who ruined my life.

Who also happens to be a professional tiler.

* * *

John Dean swept me off my size sixes when I was just coming to the end of my first year at university. I thought I had the whole world at my feet. The university was really only a glorified polytechnic, and I was only studying Business and Marketing so I wasn't as exposed to the full-on student thing as if I'd been reading Philosophy or something at a proper university. But even though it was no more than twenty miles from Milton Keynes I made the decision to leave home and rent a room in a suitably run-down, three-storey townhouse, with arty posters on the walls, tasselled scarves over lampshades, and piles of unwashed dishes in the sink. Glorious!

Most evenings, my friends and I would stroll down to the student nights at the studenty bars and hang out with the real students. But after a while, I saw through them completely and decided they were a bunch of self-important idiots. So when John Dean walked into my life one night, with his posse of slick out-on-the-pull guys and his killer smile, I was a gonner. He seemed so real, so down to earth, so normal.

Yeah, right.

My morals had gone out the window with my virginity two years before, so it was no big deal when we fell into bed on our first date: his bed, in his rented one-storey house with a

97

tin roof in Beanhill. The rest is ancient history.

Or at least, I thought it was history. But here he is now on my doorstep, my still-in-need-of-fixing doorstep, with a face like a fallen angel and that look I know so well.

I hate myself for admitting this, I really do, but when I open the door and see him standing there I fly back through time and I'm nineteen again, and he's twenty-two and totally, unforgivingly gorgeous.

'Stella,' he drawls – no, really, I mean it. He does drawl. He's one of those guys for whom the word languid was invented.

'Bloody hell,' I reply in a not very ladylike or cool way.

'How are you?' he says.

'Get lost,' I tell him and slam the door in his face.

This may seem impolite but you don't know what he did to me and Lipsy. You *think* you know: the old story of boy meets girl, boy gets girl pregnant, boy ditches girl and leaves her to bring up the baby alone.

Essentially this is all true, but there was so much more to it than that. John Dean didn't just break my heart when he deserted, abandoned, dumped me. He left my entire being broken, incapable of trusting another man or forming another relationship for years and years. John Dean used up every cliché in the book. He slept with not just one of my friends but three – and I only had three. He dumped me and came back so many times I felt like I had a revolving door in my room. Lying to me, taking money from me, using my name to get credit then leaving me to pay it all off – you name it, he did it.

Finally, he went for good, three weeks before Lipsy was born, and Lipsy and I didn't see him until she was ten. Ten! Then he turns up at my parents' house with a story of regret and a toy more suitable for a five-year-old boy. Come to think of it, I don't suppose he even knew the sex of his child, even though I'd written letter after letter for the first couple of years to the forwarding address he left with his landlord.

But I'm not bitter.

I've come to terms with it now. I accept that it was partly my fault. I was too young and naive, and far too much in love with him. That kind of love, I've decided, is dangerous. The kind that leaves you breathless and helpless, and definitely brainless in my case. He won't have that effect on me now; there's not even the slightest possibility that I'd fall for it again. Absolutely not one.

Still, I'm not taking any chances.

'Get lost,' I say again as he pushes open the letterbox.

'Stella. Come on sweetheart, don't be that way. I just want to talk to you. About Lipsy.'

The fact is that even though he and my daughter have forged some kind of relationship over the last few years, I've managed to avoid laying eyes on him. She was old enough to meet up with him herself by the time he bothered to show any interest, and both of them seemed to prefer it that way, as if they sensed that my feelings for him would poison everything and get in the way. I didn't even mind her staying over occasionally. I told myself it was good for her to have a father figure, even one like him, and that although he'd treated me badly that didn't mean I should stand in their way now.

Of course, that backfired in my face big time, giving my oh-so-clever daughter the opportunity she needed to pull the wool over my eyes and pretend she was visiting her father when all the time she was with that Robert bloke. I must have mug written all over my face.

He puts his hand inside the letterbox, trying to open it further and get a better view. I have an irresistible urge to slam the cover down on his hand – so I do just that, hoping to sever at least one finger.

'Ow! What the hell was that for? Come on, Stella, don't be like this. We need to talk about our daughter.'

It is his use of the words "our daughter" that makes me fling open the door and confront him. Except he is still somehow attached to the door and as it flies open he falls off balance and lands on his arse in a pile of rotten, soggy rubbish. What a joyous sight.

'You've got a bloody cheek, John Dean, coming here to my house and talking about *our* daughter. God, you've only known her for five minutes and already you want to tell me how to bring her up. What a nerve! You're nothing to this family. Nothing you say is of any interest to me and if you don't get off my property in ten seconds I'm calling the police. You're scum and I hate you and I never want to see you again.'

Boy, have I waited a long time to say that. Oh yes. It feels good.

For about thirty seconds. And then I realise my ex has extricated himself from the rubbish pile and is regarding me with laughing eyes.

'Oh,' I say. 'Do I *amuse* you?'

'No,' he tells me but his eyes say otherwise. Now I look more closely I see that they actually have crow's feet spidering out from the corners and that his wide mouth is also quite heavily lined. Looks like he's still a heavy smoker. Those eyes are, come to mention it, a bit watery. Maybe a heavy drinker still too.

Seventeen years. Written all over his face. I wonder whether mine has aged as badly but I think (hope?) not. Women have a better deal in that regard. So many potions and lotions out there – and I've used most of them. Make-up helps, of course. And in my case, sensible, restrained living. Which wasn't through choice so much as lack of opportunity but hey, I'm reaping the rewards now.

My anger drains away. I leave the door open and retreat down the hallway towards the kitchen. In there I find the kettle and fill it with water, my actions automatic, the polite hostess.

'Tea?' I ask when I feel him in the room behind me.

I don't turn around.

Chapter 11

Paul

Paul considered his options carefully. The young assistant, popping chewing gum all the way, had helpfully guided him to the right section of the store and pointed out which toys might be suitable for an eight-year-old girl. Still, he was stumped. A dazzling display of dolls stretched out into the distance, each more elaborately complicated than the one before. This doll, for example, had a strangely large head and what looked like an entire social network of friend-dolls. The one opposite had a boyfriend called Jessie and sported outrageously improbable proportions. Not good for young girls, surely? Or boys for that matter.

What if Hannah wasn't even into dolls? What if she was a tomboy type and preferred chemistry sets or toy guns? He didn't even know if kids her age actually played with toys anymore; wasn't it all computer games and virtual reality now?

The only person he could think of to ask was the one person he couldn't talk to about Hannah at the moment. Which was very inconvenient. He could understand that Stella wanted to protect him, it was what friends did. But her timing was terrible.

Settling on the easy option of a jigsaw puzzle, Paul paid and left the store, checking his watch for the hundredth time that morning. He'd taken too long – now he'd have to floor it to get to Dunstable by twelve. He also knew he shouldn't have spent so long deciding what to wear – she was only eight, for pity's sake – but he wanted to make the right impression. First impressions count, even for kids. *Especially* for kids.

The house was a double-fronted Georgian on a sleepy, tree-lined street. Paul hadn't expected Sharon to live somewhere so grand. He parked haphazardly and grabbed Hannah's puzzle and the chocolates he'd brought for her mum. (God, how inadequate was that? Sorry I ruined your life but here, have some Quality Street.)

A man answered the door. Paul hadn't expected that either.

'You must be Paul,' the man said. He was in his late forties, shaved head, barrel-chested and squat.

'That's right.' Paul forced himself to smile. It wasn't returned.

'Come in.'

Paul followed him into the house and down a wide hall into what must have been some kind of family room. Toys – mainly dolls – littered the floor, along with a hundred-weight of computer games and at least three consoles. The decor, Paul noticed with his estate agent's eye, was expensive and classy. There was clearly money here. Not that it was any of his business. Paul sat down on the edge of a sofa, smoothing his artfully distressed jeans with hot hands.

The man had disappeared without a word. He returned moments later leading a small, round-faced girl behind him. Not a girl – an angel. Shoulder-length curly blonde hair shone as if freshly brushed. Her skin looked like a porcelain doll's, punctuated by the biggest, bluest eyes Paul had ever seen. She seemed a little shy – understandably – and stood with one leg twisted behind the other, twirling the edge of her sleeve.

Over the last few days, Paul had allowed himself to indulge in dreams of what his daughter might look like, and in those dreams she had looked exactly like this. She was

102

almost too perfect, as if someone had reached into his mind and created her from his thoughts. There was no doubt that this was his child. Hannah had his hair, his eyes. And now his heart.

Paul looked up at the man. 'Does she know who I am?'

The man turned to Hannah. 'This is Paul,' he said. 'He's a friend of your mum's. I'll be back soon.'

So the child didn't know who he was yet. He supposed that was OK. Sharon would want to see that he was serious about getting involved in Hannah's life before she told her. But she looked so timid and scared, being left alone with a stranger, that Paul silently cursed the man he could only assume was Sharon's partner for not making more of an effort to put the child at ease.

Kneeling, Paul picked up the nearest doll, recognising it from his shopping trip earlier.

'Now this one,' he said, as if to himself, 'has her own car, I'm sure. I wonder where it is? I think…' He pretended to look through one of the piles of plastic. 'I think it was red.'

'Pink,' came a tiny voice close to his head. A pale hand reached into the mêlée and pulled out a miniature pink Porsche-alike.

'Pink!' Paul said. 'Of course, that's what I thought.'

Hannah sat splay-legged and thrust the doll into the car. 'She wants to go to the cinema,' she said, speaking more clearly this time.

'OK…'

'And so do I.'

Paul smiled. All the women he'd ever met were good at getting what they wanted, and this little one was no exception.

'Well, next time I visit maybe I could take you to the cinema. What film would you like to see?'

Hannah hid her face, suddenly shy again. Paul returned to the doll, placing her hands on the steering wheel just so and making her drive erratically around the floor, complete with sound effects. His daughter watched warily out of enormous eyes, opening her mouth a little whenever he looked likely to crash her precious doll into the wall or a piece of furniture.

'Where is your mummy?' Paul asked after a while. He could tell Hannah was starting to relax around him. The more he looked at her the more he could see the resemblance to Sharon too, and he wondered if she would have changed much since their last meeting almost nine years ago. And whether she had forgiven him.

'I'm here,' came a voice from the doorway.

'Sharon!' Paul jumped to his feet and then hesitated, not sure whether to hold out his hand or his arms for a hug. What was appropriate for a meeting of parents after nine years apart?

'Hello, Paul.' Sharon smiled and resolved the problem by holding out her hand, shaking his calmly and then crouching on the floor to embrace Hannah. 'Have you been a good girl?' she said to her daughter, laughing when Hannah nodded solemnly.

'We've been playing with her car,' Paul said, searching his mind for something more adequate to say. The situation felt unreal. He had no idea what to do next.

'You boys!' Sharon laughed. 'In a room full of girl's toys you'll always find the car to play with.'

Paul laughed too, some of the tension leaving him. He couldn't believe how little Sharon had changed, and he told her so.

'Oh, come off it,' she said with a wave of her hand. 'I look aeons older.' But she seemed pleased with the compliment all the same.

Hannah was clamouring for her mum's attention and they made their way to the kitchen where Sharon started to make lunch. There was no sign of the man Paul had met earlier.

Once Hannah was engrossed in her meal of turkey sandwiches and cherry tomatoes, Sharon turned to Paul. 'Would you like to go out into the garden so we can talk properly? I'll ask Sam to keep an eye on Hannah.' Paul nodded mutely and waited while Sharon disappeared into the house to find the mysterious Sam.

They sat on a painted white bench in the shade of a willow tree, at the end of an enormous garden.

'You have an amazing house,' Paul said, looking out across the manicured lawn and topiary hedges. 'And a beautiful garden.'

'Sam loves gardening,' Sharon replied, sipping from a glass of water and then setting it down by her feet. She turned to face him. 'I hope you don't mind that I didn't come and say hello straight away. I thought you might like to spend a little time with Hannah first. In case you found it awkward, seeing me again.'

Paul thought back to their last meeting, their last argument. He could understand why she might think that, but he set her mind at rest immediately.

'It's all in the past now. And it's all pretty fuzzy, to be honest. What matters is here and now – and what matters most of all is Hannah.'

Sharon smiled. 'She is a treasure, isn't she? Were you surprised by how much she looks like you?'

Paul nodded. 'A little. She looks like you, too. She's just perfect.'

'Some men,' Sharon said softly, 'would have been suspicious. Some might have doubted just my word after all this time.'

Paul shook his head firmly. 'I know Hannah's mine. And why would you lie, anyway? It's obvious you don't need money.' He waved his hand at the huge house and garden. 'There's nothing I could offer her that she doesn't already have.'

'Except a father.' Sharon said. 'And that counts for a lot.'

'Yes,' he agreed. 'It does.'

'But if you wanted a paternity test I'd understand. I wouldn't hold it against you.'

'No!' Paul said sharply, making Sharon jump. He thought about how he'd lain in bed last night and wondered whether Stella was right to be dubious, whether he should be more suspicious himself and ask for proof. Now all that seemed ridiculous and disloyal.

'I have her birth certificate here,' Sharon said, pulling a piece of paper from her pocket and handing it to Paul. 'The dates match up, Paul. We were away together for two weeks when she was conceived. Do you remember that? There's no way she could be anyone else's.' She pushed the paper into his hands, sweeping away his refusal.

Paul looked at the date of birth with only half his attention. The other half was reliving the memory of that fortnight's holiday in Scotland. It was one of the reasons they'd ultimately split: two weeks of relentlessly facing the fact that they had nothing in common. Except for the sex. There had been a lot of sex, and the thought of it now – and the idea that Hannah had been conceived in such a passionate and energetic way – made him smile. Sharon noticed and smiled too.

'We had a good time, didn't we?'

'Yes, we did.' Paul hoped she was remembering the good bits and not the rows and the harsh words, or how painful it had all become in the end. But then didn't every relationship that ended at all end in a painful way? Was there any chance of moving on in your life minus another person without experiencing pain and heartbreak? And, if he was honest, wasn't that one of the reasons he avoided relationships so assiduously now?

'So what do you want to do?' Sharon was asking him.

'About Hannah, you mean?' he said. Sharon nodded. 'Well, I definitely want to be in her life. If she wants that too – if you do, I mean. I want to be her father. Is that OK?' he asked, suddenly unsure. Sharon might have been hoping for more, her memories skewed by the passing of time.

But she was nodding vigorously. 'That's more than OK.

That's brilliant. She's been asking questions lately, awkward ones, you know? It will be so good for her to have a man in her life – not just a father figure but her actual father.' She smiled and Paul smiled back, warily.

'Won't your, um, your fella mind about me being on the scene?'

'Fella?' Sharon looked puzzled for a moment then her face cleared and she laughed. 'Oh, you mean Sam. He's not my fella, silly. You don't remember him, do you? Come to think of it, you only met once, and he – unlike you – has changed a lot over the years. Sam isn't my partner, Paul. He's my brother.'

* * *

Later, sitting in traffic on the interminable A5, Paul thought back to Sam's cool welcome. He was quite right to be protective of his sister. Paul knew it would take a while to prove he was around for good now, but he was determined to make a friend of Sam one day.

Just as he was determined to be the best possible dad to Hannah – and to make up for missing the first eight years of her life. Sharon had seemed genuinely sorry for keeping Hannah a secret, but Paul told her he understood, and he meant it. There was no point dwelling on the past now. They had to move on and think about the future. He had a daughter. A beautiful, clever, special daughter. Paul could hardly believe how much his life had changed over the last few days. Couldn't believe how only a week ago the most important thing on his mind had been arranging a game of squash.

He laughed to himself, and noticed how the laugh sounded a little hollow. So much for wanting to be a bachelor forever. So much for never wanting the burden of kids. Even though he hadn't consciously chosen it, he wouldn't change the situation for the world now. He had felt such a bond with

Hannah, such a connection, that he couldn't imagine a future without her. His mind was filled with plans – places he could take her, things they could do together, the fun they would have. He was a dad. His whole life had been turned upside down and he was loving every minute of it.

Chapter 12

Stella

CAN'T LIVE WITHOUT
American double-door ice-maker fridge-freezer
Kenwood food mixer
Cath Kidston Kitchenalia
Furniture! (Sofa, dining table, chairs, beds,
    wardrobes…)
Clothes: see sub-list
TV
Lipsy - computer, Playstation, iPod, clothes…
Carpets for entire house
New bathroom suite and towels ✓
Tiling - bathroom and kitchen
Bed linen x 4 - Marks & Spencer

When I look at the list again on my break a few days later, I notice that my objects of desire are getting more and more practical as time goes on. I suppose this was to be expected, but it makes me feel further away from all the things that mean something to me, those little luxuries that make me sure of my place in the world. But I guess first I will have to find the money for carpets and paint and boring things like sheets and duvets – not to mention pans and plates and tea towels and lampshades and curtains and on and on …

All those things we simply accumulate without realising it

throughout our lives. I never realised how much stuff I had until it was all gone. To put the contents of an entire house back together again is a mammoth task and one I am feeling more and more fazed by every day. As fast as the money comes in – which isn't fast at all, let's face it – it goes out again on mere essentials. This is a soul-destroying process.

And then there's my job at Café Crème. The work's OK, and the customers aren't too bad, and the boss isn't around too often. Gina and I have a laugh, which is something I sorely need at the moment. It's fun to work with a laid-back woman – she's restored my faith in female colleagues after too many brushes with Loretta.

But the hours are killing me. I hardly get any time to see Lipsy, who's becoming more distant every day. And during the little time I do have left, I don't have the energy for decorating or cleaning.

Joshua seems happy enough to help with the cleaning.

And who is tiling my bathroom? Right now as I stare out of the window when I should be typing up rental agreements? Hmm, I have to confess. It's John Dean.

Don't judge me too harshly – I've already had that particular lecture from Bonnie. The way I figure it is, he owes me big time and I really need someone to do my tiling, so what's the problem? He's just a resource I'm using, that's all. I'm using lots of resources at the moment: Joshua's organising and cleaning abilities, my mother's laundry services, my newlywed neighbours' microwave for those handy little meals-in-a-box I'm reduced to living off, and the painting skills of anyone who offers.

So why not the tiling abilities of my long-ago ex? What could possibly go wrong?

***

I wait out the rest of the afternoon and then escape into the late evening sunshine with the last of the shoppers. Milton

110

Keynes' shopping centre is a beautiful place as the sun goes down – all sparkling glass and soft blue lighting. I'm at a loose end tonight. No shift at Café Crème, thank the Lord. The decorating is at a bit of an impasse until payday, and Bonnie is playing happy families with Marcus and Cory. Lipsy is probably in the arms of pseudo father figure, Robert, and Paul – well, things haven't improved much since I cast doubt on Hannah's paternity. Not to mention my faux pas. Why couldn't I just leave well alone?

With limited choices – and the option of a night in my house alone with no sofa, TV or food not that attractive – I decide to visit my mother. When I arrive at the house I'm surprised to find it empty. No big shock that my daughter's not here, just a sad jolt when I realise that every conversation I've had with her recently has involved me giving her some kind of lecture and her telling me she hates me and I've ruined her life. Such is parenthood. It is a joy to find that Alistair's out, and I waste no time in ensconcing myself on the squashy sofa with a big bowl of crisps and an EastEnders repeat on the telly.

Mum comes in at half ten.

'Where've you been?' I ask her, my tone just this side of accusatory.

'Nowhere!' she says too quickly, which I think makes her sound guilty but what on earth could my mother have done to be guilty about?

I pat the seat next to me and she perches on it warily.

'I came round to see you,' I tell her, waiting for the outburst of gratitude.

'Did you?' She fiddles with her handbag, which I've only just noticed is still clutched on her lap and not thrown on the stairs as usual.

'Yes, I did.' This conversation is getting us nowhere. 'Would you like a cup of tea, Mum?' I say, standing.

'I'll do it.'

She stands too, and we jostle our way to the kitchen, each

protesting that they should make the tea and the other should sit down. In my case it's because I really want to do something nice for her – she seems a bit stressed, and in my mother, this is not a good thing. Spending quickly follows stress, unnecessary items piling up around the house like little trophies from her struggle against the vagaries of disappointment.

In her case, I get the feeling she just wants to get me out of the way, so I stay and hover and watch her like a hawk, asking questions one after the other in a constant stream: 'Are you OK, Mum? Where have you been today, Mum? Why are you acting so weird, Mum?'

It isn't long before she cracks.

'I've been to see your father, OK!' she snaps.

'Well,' I say, in true face the music fashion, 'I'd better get off now. Early start tomorrow.'

'Stella, wait!' She grabs my arm and we both look at her hand in silence for a few seconds. 'Please wait a minute. There's something I have to tell you.'

'Not listening!' I don't actually put my fingers in my ears, but the resemblance to a child is hard even for me to ignore.

'Oh, for goodness sake, Stella. You're going to have to talk about it sooner or later. He's coming out in a few months, he'll be back here large as life and what will you do then? Ignore us all?'

'If I have to, yes.'

'Well, that's impossible. And I know you won't do it, if only for Lipsy's sake.'

Damn it but she's right. Lipsy loves her granddad; she was more upset than anyone when he went to prison and her behaviour problems started soon after, which is yet another thing I blame him for.

'So?' I say, sounding a lot like my own stroppy teenager.

My mother walks across the kitchen and opens her bag. 'So,' she says, turning to me again. 'You have to face up to it. You have to stop hiding and face him. And the only way you

112

can do that, Stella, is by going to see him yourself.'

'Fat chance!'

'I just can't talk to you when you're like this, I never could. It makes me laugh when you have a go at Lipsy. If only you could see how much she takes after her mother. Here.' She takes a letter out of her bag, walks back to me and pushes it into my hand. 'Take this and go home.'

I look at the envelope, and although I know exactly what it is, I say, 'What is this?'

My mother shakes her head. 'Just go home, Stella.'

Which is, I could have told her, what I wanted all along.

* * *

Lipsy

Friday 6th July

Things I Can't Possibly Live Without:
My own space; Rob; my diaries; access to the internet – preferably on my own computer; insurance against fire – and water, and whatever else could happen; my grandma; my granddad; a belly button ring...

Lipsy tapped her teeth while she considered her latest diary entry. She'd been rewriting her list weekly, although it had never really changed much from the first one she'd written. This last item, though – she wasn't so sure about that. It had been Rosie's idea. That they should go together to the tattoo shop in Stony Stratford and have matching piercings. It would be a massive laugh, Rosie said.

'Maybe,' Lipsy had answered. 'But not matching. That's a bit sad, don't you think?'

Rosie agreed vigorously. 'Whatever. My mum will go ballistic.'

The thought of mums going ballistic might appeal to her

friend, but Lipsy had had enough of maternal warfare recently. And it seemed to never end either – even her mother and her grandma were at each other's throats when they should be acting like grown-ups and sorting things out properly.

Take last night. Lipsy had been creeping in the door around eleven o'clock – only just past the hour her grandma considered an appropriate time for nearly-eighteen-year-olds to come home, but enough past to warrant the creeping. As she passed the kitchen she heard voices and stopped to listen, thinking it might be Alistair with a girlfriend.

She was disappointed, and then a bit worried, to recognise her mother's voice. Dropping her jacket and her bag silently to the floor and slipping off her shoes (she could always pretend she'd been in for ages if she was caught), Lipsy moved closer until her ear was pressed against the wooden door.

Her grandma's voice was raised, which was pretty unusual in itself, and then she distinctly heard her mother say, 'Oh, get a life, will you?' Lipsy clapped her hand over her mouth to stop herself from laughing. Her mum sounded like a teenager. But a really uncool one.

'I have one, madam, unlike some. You'd do better than to look down your nose at me. One day…' Her grandma's voice lowered so Lipsy couldn't make out what she said next, but she could well imagine, having been on the receiving end of similar lectures herself from both of them – but mostly from her mother. She didn't know whether to feel sorry for her mum or not. That would depend on what they were arguing about.

She held her breath and strained to sort the murmuring into separate words. "Betrayal" was one, and "Selfish" was another, but who said what was hard to determine. Then she heard her grandma's voice clearly again.

'*When* he comes out, not if,' she said, her voice loud but thick with emotion. Sure enough, Lipsy could make out the unmistakeable sounds of crying soon after.

114

So that was it. They were arguing about her granddad. Lipsy had crept away as quietly as she could. She missed him, and nobody ever talked about him in front of her. It was as if the event – and the man himself – had been wiped out of existence. Even though Lipsy knew her grandma went to visit him once a month, she didn't feel she could ask about it in case it made her sad.

Nobody had ever asked her if she wanted to go.

Lipsy shook her head now and turned back to her latest diary entry. The one thing she wanted to write, even more than her list of important stuff, was that she had come on her period and all was well. But unfortunately she couldn't. This was causing her more and more anxiety every day that passed – an anxiety that she tried to hide but which was gnawing its way up through her belly and into her throat. Soon she'd have to tell Rob. What would he say? Would he blame her and never want to see her again? And what would she do then? Never mind what her mum would say. She didn't even want to *think* about that.

Chapter 13

Paul

Paul hadn't spent as long choosing what to wear for his drink with Stella as he had the day he'd gone to meet Hannah for the first time. In fact, he hadn't spent any time at all. If the truth be told, he wasn't looking forward to the evening as much as he would have a few weeks ago. Things had been so strained between them since the day Stella had made what he could only call a pass at him, despite their mutual assurances that nothing would change.

It was a shame. He hadn't realised how much he valued her friendship until he started to feel it slipping away. Especially now he had Hannah, had something special to share, and no one to share it with.

'You look nice,' Stella said when he arrived.

Paul looked down at his T-shirt guiltily, noticing how faded and scruffy it was, and suddenly wishing he'd made more of an effort. Stella looked stunning, as usual. She didn't seem to mind, though. She merely slipped her arm through his and pushed through the double doors into the pub as if it was the most natural thing in the world.

Which it was. This was how they would walk down the street if they went shopping or out for lunch. Stella was fairly demonstrative but he'd never taken it to mean anything special. Until now. Now he found himself unconsciously analysing her every touch and gesture to see if they contained a deeper meaning.

'You look nice too,' he told her, adjusting to the noise level inside the pub. Even in her thirties, Stella turned heads wherever she went. It used to make Paul proud of her, the way a brother feels proud of his little sister. Now, for some inexplicable reason, it made him nervous.

They picked out a table and Paul, feeling ridiculously self-conscious, went to the bar. A hundred times we've done this, he told himself, a hundred times we've been here, or to bars like this, and chatted and laughed and chatted some more. Paul was starting to wish that he could go back in time two weeks and wipe away what had happened. It just seemed as if since then everything that was usually smooth and easy between them had become hard work.

Before, he could say anything to her. Like: *You really upset me, Stella, when you suggested Hannah might not be mine, and now I think about it every time I see you.*

But now it was impossible to say something like that without feeling as though he was crossing some invisible line. And she was definitely more touchy. He wasn't imagining that.

He watched her now out of the corner of his eye, playing with the beer mats, ripping little slits in them and trying to construct some kind of tower. Paul also noticed three lads in their late twenties eyeing her openly, one of them smoothing his hair back in a completely affected way, trying to get her attention. He paid for their drinks and hurried back.

'So,' he said, trying to sound upbeat. 'What's new?'

'God, you'll never guess. My bloody mother only wants me to go and see my dad.' That was Stella – straight into it, no preamble, no messing about.

'Wow!' Paul leaned across the table to block the view of the three lads. 'What did you say?'

'Oh, I said "Yes, Mummy, of course I'll go. What time would he like me to get there?" What do you think I said, you idiot? I told her to get stuffed.'

118

Paul readjusted to this suddenly angry Stella. 'Good, good. Well, let's hope she leaves it alone now, eh?'

She leaned back in her chair, leaving a pile of decimated beer mats behind. 'Yeah, I guess. Although, really, it's not as easy as that, is it?'

'No. I don't suppose it is.'

'I mean, he's going to be out soon. Did you know that? He's going to be out and coming home to my mother, living in what is, after all, still his house. Even though they had to remortgage it to pay off the fine and court costs, and even though she's had no support ever since. It's still his house.'

'Yeah, that's true.' Paul sipped his drink and nodded warily.

'And, even though I don't want anything to do with him, if my daughter decides to stay in that house, which I can't stop her doing now she's nearly-eighteen – as she so loves to remind me – I'll have to face him sooner or later.'

She was warming up now, hair flicked back in irritation, long fingers tapping on the table. Paul longed to look round and gauge the lads' reaction to her – Stella was even more beautiful when she was fired up like this – but he didn't dare in case she noticed and thought he wasn't listening.

'Well,' she was saying, 'what do you think?'

'I think,' he said carefully, 'that you should do whatever feels right for you.'

'Oh, you're right.' She reached across the table and squeezed his hand. 'The thing is, Paul, I'm not sure I do know what feels right for me. I've spent so long feeling angry with him, for leaving us, for causing such a huge big mess, it's impossible to think about it logically now. Will you help me?'

The look on her face was just like the old Stella, and he chided himself for being paranoid. So what if she had made a pass at him – he should be grateful, not freaked out. Look at the way those lads were eyeing her. She was a real catch, was Stella, and here he was, having a drink with her, sharing her problems and her worries, holding her hand...

119

If anything, he should consider himself lucky. Very lucky indeed.

What was his problem?

'Will you help me, Paul?' Stella said again, her eyes big and pleading. And suddenly, with all the subtlety of a concrete block falling from a crane, Paul knew exactly what his problem was.

His problem was Stella. Beautiful, passionate, funny, clever, crazy Stella. Why was he so jealous of those guys eyeing her up? Why was he so protective of her with his mates, and with every bloke she'd ever dated? Why did he always drop everything to help her out if she needed him? Why did he think (hope) it was her every time his phone rang? Why did he hate John Dean so much? And why, oh why, had he never noticed it before?

He thought about Hannah and about what it meant to him – having a child, being a parent – and he realised for the first time how empty his life was. He'd been hiding from it for a long time, too scared to open up and risk letting someone become close. But someone had been close all along. He'd just refused to admit it – to himself or to her.

Stella was still looking at him questioningly. He gripped her hand with both of his and forgot the three lads with their smoothed-back hair, and forgot he'd ever been angry over what she'd said about Hannah. All he could think about was the way her lips had felt on his and how much he wanted it to happen again.

He knew why he'd been feeling so awkward around her lately, and why their relationship felt so different, so altered.

He'd built a wall up around himself, so thick and strong it had taken someone like Stella to knock it down. No one else could have done it. No one else would have stood a chance.

He gazed into her eyes now and felt the rest of the world fading away. 'Of course I'll help you, Stella,' he said. 'Let's go through it one step at a time. Together.'

Three pints of lager and three white wines later and Paul was sitting on Stella's side of the table with her head on his shoulder, a mixture of her tears and a healthy serving of snot making a damp patch on his T-shirt. This is love, Paul thought hazily. He wasn't drunk exactly, he just had that slightly detached feeling – detached, that is, from all the inconsequential things which usually bothered him. It felt liberating. He should do it more often.

They'd talked about her father, about her feelings and her anger and disappointment. Paul had counselled her to go and visit the man in prison. He knew it was the right thing to do, and he knew it was what she wanted. She just didn't want to admit it, not after all this time. She was proud like that. He hoped they would be reconciled; he wanted everything in her life to be perfect for her.

And he desperately wanted her to notice him again.

Stella, wiping her nose on the back of her hand, sat up suddenly and peered at her drink. 'S'empty,' she slurred.

Stella *was* drunk. Paul had seen her three sheets to the wind enough times to know the signs, not that they were too hard to read: the slurring, the glazed eyes, the overflowing of emotion when normally she was quite guarded in that department. Not that he minded, far from it. In fact, he was starting to think that this might be the perfect opportunity to return her pass with one of his own. Not in a taking advantage kind of way, of course. He wasn't planning on trying to get her into bed or anything. Nice though the idea was now that it appeared in his head in all its naked glory…

No! Bad thinking, Smart. Not very smart at all. Probably better to wait until she's sober and you can both at least remember how great it was.

'Drink!' Stella said again, pushing her empty glass across the table, which was now completely littered with pieces of beer mat as well as a large number of wet tissues.

'I think you might have had enough to drink, madam,' he told her. 'Unless you fancy an orange juice.'

'Spoilsport.' She pulled her face into a sulk. It was very sexy. Paul put his arm around her shoulders again. It felt so natural, so right.

'Stella,' he began softly, 'I've been thinking. About us.'

'Mmm?' She nestled closer. He wished those three lads hadn't left half an hour ago and that they were still here to see this.

'About what happened that day. You know, when you, when you tried to, erm, kiss me. I know that we haven't really mentioned it since and that our friendship is the most important thing to both of us but I think that –'

Stella sat up suddenly, pulling his hand off her shoulder and gripping it tightly. 'It's OK, Paul,' she said, trying to focus her eyes on his, failing, and then trying again. 'I know what you're going to say.'

'You do?'

'Yes.' She nodded vigorously. 'You're going to say that I shouldn't have done it and that we should stay as friends, because if we didn't have our friendship what would we have? And you're right. You're absolutely right, Paul Smart. You really are very, very smart, Mr Smart.' She collapsed into giggles.

Paul shook his head. No, that wasn't what he was going to say at all. He had to put her right. He opened his mouth to speak but she was off again.

'And the thing is,' she said loudly, pointing her finger at herself, 'I'm actually rubbish at relationships anyway. So it's just as well you knocked me back. Look at my track record. It's like a disaster movie.'

Paul had to admit that Stella's rare forays into the world of love had more often than not ended pretty badly. From that loser John Dean onwards every man she'd dated had turned out to be wrong for her in more ways than you could name. Even her most recent beau, the slimy Joshua, had revealed himself to be an obsessive-compulsive who only wanted to tell her the best way to live her life – his way, of course. Stella wouldn't hear a word against him though, said he was being a "good friend". Ha!

But he didn't want to think about that now. He needed to shut her up and get back to talking about them. Unfortunately, she was on a roll and all he could do was listen.

'And I need all the friends I can get, Paul, I really do. Because I'm at one of those points in my life where I'm feeling so confused. I know you're confused too, about Hannah and everything. So I understand, you see, that you want to leave things the way they are between us and just be friends.'

'Yes, but I–'

'Because we're *real* friends and there's nothing can get in the way of that. Is there?' She didn't give him a chance to answer, just carried on over him, twisting her hair into a ball on top of her head as she talked. Her eyes were smudged from crying, with little rivers of dried tears streaking down her face. Paul wanted to kiss them off one by one.

'I'm just so confused,' she said again. 'I mean, he comes back into my life just when I think I'm getting myself all sorted out. He comes back into my life like nothing's ever happened and I'm supposed to just forgive him, am I? Just say, "Oh, hello, come in, how've you been? What did you do with your life after ruining mine?"'

Paul figured he'd lost track of this conversation somewhere along the line. Who the hell was she talking about? He'd thought they were talking about whether they should stay friends or become more than that. He stopped her hands from twisting, held them in his, and made her face him again.

'What are you going on about, Stella? Forgive who?'

'Bloody John Dean, that's who. Oh, he knows exactly the effect he has on me, always has. But I won't fall for it again. I just won't. You won't let me, will you, Paul? You'll help me to

123

resist him.'

Paul slumped back in his chair, feeling the hard wooden slats dig into his spine. The fog around his head was starting to clear, and he felt himself sobering up very quickly.

So that was it. John Dean was back on the scene. Sounded like a poem, he thought. A sick, twisted poem. Stella had been a sucker for that lowlife since the first day she'd met him. How could he compete with that, compete with the father of her child? Should he even try, for that matter? But surely she wouldn't be tempted, not after everything the man had put her through? Stella was far too switched on for that. Wasn't she?

Suddenly Paul felt slightly sick, the effects of the alcohol wearing off too quickly and leaving him with nothing but an early hangover. For a brief moment, it had all seemed so perfect – Stella liked him, he liked Stella, what could be more simple? Now he had to face the very unpleasant thought that he might have blown it after all. He'd left it too late. She'd changed her mind. And now he had the inimitable John Dean to contend with.

This was not good at all.

Chapter 14

Lipsy

Lipsy stood outside Café Crème and steeled herself for the ordeal to come. Today, to make the right impression and to give herself the best chance of a good outcome, she had left her hair slightly wavy, the way her mother liked it, not straightened to within an inch of its life. She'd also worn jeans and a top which covered up her midriff; now was not the time to go showing off her new, and very sore, belly button ring.

Walking into the coffee shop, she spotted her mum straight away, the bright yellow uniform setting off her long dark hair and olive skin. Lipsy had always wished she'd been blessed with her mother's colouring. She had the hair but her own skin was pale – pale and interesting, her grandma said, but that was only to make her feel better about looking like a ghost most of the time. When she'd first met her father a couple of years ago, Lipsy saw that it was him she took after in the looks department. Her mother had never mentioned that.

'Lipsy, hey!' Her mum called her over to the counter and she trailed across the room dutifully. 'This is a nice surprise. Meeting Rosie?'

Lipsy shook her head. 'No, I'm not.'

'Not Robert is it?'

'No, Mum,' Lipsy said wearily. She decided to let it go for now, as there were bigger issues to discuss. But her mum

125

wouldn't be able to ignore him forever. Especially not now.

'Have you come to see me?' Her mother laughed as if this was a silly thing to say and then looked ridiculously pleased when Lipsy told her, Yes, she had.

'Grab that table then and I'll get us some lattes. I'm due a break soon anyway.'

Lipsy wandered over to a corner table, positioning the chairs so that her mum would be sitting with her back to the counter. This was the least she could do, she thought. Protect her from prying eyes. She was pleased with herself for being so thoughtful.

'Are you sure it's OK to have a break?' Lipsy asked when her mum sat down.

'God, yes. I deserve one,' she said, yawning.

They sipped their coffees and stared around the café in a silence that was, if not exactly companionable, at least not too awkward.

'How are things?' Lipsy asked. As she'd instigated this meeting she might as well make the first move towards conversation.

'Not too bad. Not too bad at all, really,' her mum said, pulling a so-so face and tipping her head from side to side.

'And how's the house coming on?'

'It's good. Really good. I'm thinking of having a decorating party. You know, everyone comes round in their scruffs and brings a pot of paint and a paintbrush, and then we put some music on and have wine and nibbles. It'll be a laugh.'

Lipsy looked at her mother doubtfully. 'But what if they all bring different coloured paint? It will look crap.'

'Well, obviously it would need a bit of planning.' Her mother stirred her latte with her finger. 'It's just an idea at the moment.'

'I think it's a really good one,' Lipsy said brightly, remembering why she had come and that she needed to get her mother on side.

She racked her brains for how to start – all those carefully prepared words had disappeared the minute she sat down – but then she noticed her mother's expression. Lipsy hadn't made a habit of studying her mother's face lately; they hardly saw each other these days for one thing. But now it was just the two of them, with no distractions and no arguments (not yet, anyway), she couldn't help but notice that her mum looked sad. Really sad. And tired. And worried. She couldn't remember the last time she'd seen her look so worried.

'Are you OK, Mum? If there's anything you wanted to talk about, you know you could talk to me.' It felt good to be saying this, it felt grown-up and right somehow.

Her mother regarded her seriously for a moment or two. 'What would you say if I told you I was thinking of going to visit your granddad?'

'I'd say about time! I heard you and grandma arguing about it the other night. I wasn't eavesdropping,' she added when her mother raised her eyebrows, 'I just overheard, that's all. And, for what it's worth, I think you should go.'

'He'll be coming out soon.'

'I know.'

'How do you feel about that?'

The dreaded question. Lipsy never knew how to answer this. Often she didn't feel anything like how other people expected her to feel. 'I love Granddad,' she said simply. 'And I miss him.'

'Me too, Lipsy. Me too.' Her mother shifted her gaze off into the distance and Lipsy struggled for a way to bring her back to the present.

'How's the house coming on?' she asked.

'You're a good daughter, Lipsy,' her mother said suddenly. 'I know we've had our differences lately, and I know you blame me for the fire. No, no.' She waved away Lipsy's protestations. 'I know you do, and you're probably right to. I should have taken better care of things. At the very least I should have made sure the insurance payments were kept up.

That was unforgivable. But I'm going to make it up to you, sweetheart, I really am. I'm saving up to buy you all the things you want and I'm going to redecorate your room and make everything perfect again. You'll come home then, won't you?' she asked hopefully.

'I don't want you to buy me anything. Those kind of things aren't really what's important anyway. Actually, Mum, there's something I need to tell you. Something a bit difficult.'

But her mum was still digesting her last comment. 'But you'll want to replace all the stuff you lost, won't you? The iPod and the Playstation and the DVDs and clothes and stuff?'

'Not really. I mean, yeah, I guess so. Eventually. But it doesn't matter, does it? It was just stuff. So, anyway, I need to tell you something important.'

'Of course, go ahead.' Her mother was shaking her head as if she'd just heard something mind-blowing.

'Mum!'

'Sorry.' She leaned forward on her elbows and offered Lipsy her wide smile. 'I'm listening. Off you go.'

OK, Lipsy. Don't blow it, now. Your entire future happiness depends on how well you handle this one conversation. Nice and slowly, like we practised.

'The thing is,' Lipsy began.

'So you're really not bothered at all about any of the things you lost? You don't want to go out and replace absolutely everything bigger and better than before?'

'Mum, for God's sake, will you just listen? I'm trying to tell you something really important here and you're going on about iPods and DVDs. It's stupid, it's all just stuff. I've got bigger things to worry about now. I'm actually pregnant.'

Stunned silence, horrified expression, shaking of head.

'Yes, Mum.' Well done, Lipsy – you handled that so well. 'I'm having a baby. Rob's baby. And we're definitely going ahead with it so don't even try to talk me out of it. OK? Don't even try.'

***

Stella

Don't even try to talk me out of it, she says. As if I might march her down to the abortion clinic right there and then. Does she not realise who she is talking to? That the person sitting in front of her, although old and wrinkly now by her standards, was once in almost exactly the same situation and felt exactly the same?

I may have had a couple of years on her when I fell pregnant, but I had the very same conversation with my own mother – although maybe it was even worse for me because I also had to face my father at the same time. Their disappointment was the worst thing. I could see it washing over their faces like dirty water – our daughter, our unmarried daughter, our unmarried daughter who is going out with a feckless no-hoper, pregnant at nineteen. Career ruined. Prospects slashed. Future mapped out ahead of her like the plotline of a tacky soap.

They were crushed, both of them. At first, my dad was angry, but it didn't last long. He wasn't really angry with me anyway, although I took as much responsibility for the accident as John Dean; actually I took all the responsibility because he refused to take any. When he started to mess me about, not long into the pregnancy, my parents begged me to leave him and move back home. Those were the really big rows, the ones we hadn't had at the start because they were too shell-shocked, or too kind, to make me feel as bad about it as I maybe should have.

What goes around comes around, hey?

Now here I am, faced with an even younger pregnant daughter with even fewer prospects and even more obstacles to overcome. At least I'd already left home, and I had a modicum of an idea about how to look after myself and someone else. My boyfriend wasn't ten years older than me, although with hindsight he may have behaved more responsibly if he had been.

I know Robert isn't the problem here. The way Lipsy tells it he is being the perfect gentleman about it all, getting down on one knee to ask her to marry him (she laughed a bit too hysterically about this), looking around for a small starter home for the three of them, and putting in for a promotion at work. You have to give him credit for not running a mile – in my experience that is the norm.

No. The problem here is my sincere belief that my daughter is simply too young, physically and emotionally, to cope with having a child of her own. I have to think clearly about this and not panic. I have to be calm and sensible so I can guide her through the minefield which lies ahead. I must not panic.

Pregnant at seventeen.

Oh my God. Her life is completely ruined!

Her future's mapped out now: by twenty she'll have three children by three different fathers and be living as a single mother on the Lakes Estate, stealing formula milk from the local Co-op. And probably eking out a meagre living offering phone sex to middle-aged men in the evenings while the kids are in bed.

No. I won't let that happen.

'But you're too young to have a baby!' I screech in despair while Lipsy sits serenely taking it all in.

She takes my shaking fist in hers. 'Evidently not, as I am actually having a baby and there is nothing anybody can do about it.' She tilts her face and I notice that her cheekbones have lost some of their hollow, gothic look, and her skin is glowing. She looks radiant. How long is it since I have properly looked at my daughter, I wonder?

'How pregnant are you, exactly?'

Lipsy sits back and picks up her coffee, which is quite clearly stone cold. She shrugs.

'How long,' I say again, 'have you been pregnant?'

130

My daughter meets my eye. 'I'm not sure.'

'Well, don't you think we'd better find out?'

'I guess,' she answers sulkily.

'You're going to have to deal with it a bit more grown-up than that, young lady,' I snap back at her.

If someone had asked me yesterday how I would handle it if my daughter became pregnant, I would have told them that I'd sit down with her and discuss it calmly and maturely. I would respect her feelings. I wouldn't make any jibes or criticisms. I would be, of course, the perfect mother.

'Did you bother to think about protection at all?' I ask my daughter bluntly, not flinching when she cringes as though she'd like to disappear into her chair.

'Well, did you?'

Lipsy sinks into herself even more. She looks so small, so frail. I was a pretty strapping teenager myself, although I still provoked this same protective response in my own parents.

'I'll take that as a "no" then, shall I?' I say pompously. 'And Robert? He didn't think to use a condom?'

She became quite animated at this, defending Robert, going through the options they'd discussed, filling me in on how "amazing" he was being about it. I resisted the urge to tell her so he should be. I resisted the urge to tell her I was actually quite proud of how she was handling it. But I didn't manage to resist the urge to ask my daughter just what the hell she saw in this man in the first place. At least the master of my downfall had been devastatingly handsome.

Lipsy stares at me like I am a crazy person. 'But Rob's gorgeous. Everybody thinks so.'

I can't help wonder why she chose an older man when my daughter could have any boy in her year at school. Why him? I don't even know how they met.

And then it hits me. How can I have been so blind? I've bandied the phrase "father figure" about enough times, but the truth of it hadn't hit me until now.

How can I have missed such a classic and predictable

131

basis for a relationship? My daughter had needed a father figure for most of her life and in Robert, she'd clearly found one – a man with whom she can act out the perfect relationship, who can look after her and repair all the damage inflicted by her own lack of a father. It even explains the baby – she needs to feel needed, needs to have something that relies totally upon her. Maybe there is no question over the contraception issue, maybe this "accident" wasn't so accidental after all.

Coming to this ground-breaking conclusion does nothing to alter the facts, however. My daughter is still pregnant.

There is one person I must talk to as soon as possible, not least because I promised Lipsy that I'd be the one to tell him. I want John Dean to know exactly what he's done and what he's responsible for, however indirectly. Can I help it if the thought of seeing him – despite the amount of sheer hatred I feel for the man – fills my body with a tiny (but very exciting) electrical charge?

Chapter 15

Stella

After work on Monday I visit my mother to let her know Lipsy's news – another traumatic activity I stupidly agreed to take on. I also plan to tell her that I have decided to go and see my father. I figure that one will take the sting out of the other. I'm half right. She doesn't seem too angry about Lipsy, or disappointed even. Oddly, she blames herself.

'First you and now little Lipsy,' she wails as I try to hustle her into her favourite seat and ply her with calming camomile tea. 'And while she was under my roof as well. It's all my fault. I've let you all down.'

Now, I blame my mother for a lot of things. It can't have escaped your notice that relations are sometimes a bit strained between us. But I have never blamed my mother for my own mistakes, and I certainly won't be blaming her for Lipsy's. That's why I prepare her camomile tea now with just a little bit more care than usual, and then I sit opposite her and take both her hands in mine. I squeeze them together, telling her with as much sincerity as I can, 'Mum, it definitely isn't in any way your fault.' And then I tell her that I love her. Because, in lots of ways, I do.

It turns out that she was worried that I would think she'd encouraged it. I laugh at this – she may be more lenient as a grandma than she was as a mother, but I know for a fact she couldn't relax *that* much.

We talk about Lipsy for a while, planning her future for her the way adults do when their kids aren't around to speak up for what they want.

'I'm going to ask Lipsy to move back home,' I tell my mum. 'Not because of anything you've done,' I add as she starts wailing again. 'You've been fantastic and we're both really grateful. And, if you don't mind, I could still do with using your washing machine facilities, just until I can afford one of my own.'

'I'll buy you a washing machine,' my mother says between sniffs. 'I'd love to help out with the house.'

'I know you would, Mum. But you don't have any money, do you? You'd put it on a credit card. And then what would happen?' I don't want to be having this conversation again but why won't the woman just give it up with the buying things all the time? What is wrong with her? It's like she only gets her self-worth from spending money, from having "stuff".

Lipsy's words from yesterday come back to me, almost obliterated by everything else that came after. What had she said exactly? *It's just stuff, Mum. There are more important things in life than that.* Something along those lines. The words niggle at me but I'm not sure why. My mother could do with hearing them, though. If she wasn't feeling so vulnerable right now I might tell her.

The front door opens and slams, and my mother stiffens. 'It's Alistair,' she hisses.

Well, duh. Unless she's given a key to someone else.

He comes into the kitchen, calling, 'Hi Mags,' and then follows it with, 'Oh, Stella. You're here.' Charming.

'Actually, Alistair,' she says, 'we're in the middle of something right now. If you don't mind?'

I'm in shock. This is the first time I've seen my mother be anything other than simpering around her lodger. Alistair looks shocked too, and I watch with delight as he hovers by the doorway, clearly unwilling to be dismissed like that, especially in front of me.

I can't resist a little dig of my own. 'Run along now, there's a good boy. I'm sure you've got some games to play or something.'

He gives me a look that promises retribution and I laugh at him openly.

When he's gone I turn to my mother. 'What was all that about?'

'He's been making a bit of a nuisance of himself, I'm afraid.' She starts twirling her hair furiously. I know I should back off now but I'm hooked.

'What's he done?'

'Well, he hasn't paid his rent again. That's two months now. I know it can't go on like this, Stella. I can't have a lodger who doesn't pay any rent. So I tackled him about it a few nights ago.'

'Well done, Mum. I'm proud of you.' Atta girl.

'Mmm. It didn't go as well as I'd have liked.'

'In what way?'

My mother shifts uncomfortably. 'He, erm, he said he would pay me in kind.'

I stare at her blankly. 'Pay you in what?'

'In kind.'

In kind, I repeat internally. And then I realise what that means. 'Urghh! That's disgusting. I hope you told him where to go?'

'I most certainly did,' she says indignantly.

'Thank goodness for that.' I look closely at my mother's face. Just a little bit too uncomfortable. 'This isn't the first time it's happened, is it?'

'Actually, now you come to mention it, no it's not.'

'Oh, Mum!'

'But I told him where to go then as well. I thought he was joking. I told him, I said, "You've got to be joking." But he said he wasn't and then the other night he said it again.'

'You weren't flattered, were you?'

135

'Maybe,' she says, more than a little defensively. 'A bit, perhaps. But not really. He was just trying to get out of paying the rent, wasn't he? He doesn't fancy me. I don't suppose anyone would anymore.' She sighs, looking forlornly out of the window to the untamed wilderness beyond. I know that right now I'm supposed to bolster her ego and tell her that dad will still fancy her, but I just can't bring myself to talk about him. Not yet.

'You have to kick him out,' I tell her firmly. 'Right now. Tonight. Tell him to pack his bags and do one.'

'But I need the money, Stella. I can't manage on my own.'

Don't I bloody well know it. 'But you're not getting any money from him. That's the point. You might as well look for another lodger, give his room to someone who will actually pay you. And won't proposition you instead.'

She smiles wryly at this. 'I know, I know. You're right. I need to curb my spending and stand on my own two feet, don't I?'

'Well, yes. You do really. I wish I could help you out but I can't even afford to run my own life at the moment. I've got two jobs as it is, and I'm still struggling to do up the house. And now there's a baby on the way things are only going to get harder. Still, when…' I stop suddenly. I was about to say, 'When dad comes out,' but the words catch in my throat.

My mother pats my hand. 'I know.' Her attention wanders to the overgrown garden again and she purses her lips. 'I don't suppose you know anyone who might be up for a bit of gardening do you?'

* * *

136

Lipsy

I can't believe it's been four whole days since I last wrote in my diary. Sorry, diary, I'll make up for it now.

After telling my mother about the baby things started to get a bit weird. First of all, there was her reaction. I expected her to go ballistic – totally mental, like ground me for a century and send me away to a remedial school. But she was kind of cool about it. She made a few comments, about Rob mostly, and about me being too young. But she took it well, so well it completely freaked me out. When she asked me on Monday to move back into the house of horrors with her I just kind of said yes. Just like that. I think she was as shocked as I was.

I'm glad to be out of Gran's, though. She was weird about it, too. Crying a lot and asking me strange questions like, Where was the baby conceived? I mean – what does that matter?

So here I am, back in Crownhill, in my old room which still smells of mildew and looks like the set of a horror film. Mum's got me a new bed and we went out together to choose paint for the walls. We're going to paint it together, she says. She says it will be fun. I think she thinks it will be "bonding". At least, that's what Rosie thinks. Her mum made her take her belly ring out as soon as she'd had it done and grounded her for a month. My mum laughed when she saw mine. 'Make the most of having a nice flat belly while you can,' she said. I took it out that night.

The weirdest thing, though, is that my dad is round at the house most nights now doing odd jobs and bringing fish and chips and bottles of wine and diet coke for me. It's just freaky. Like, are they doing this for my benefit or what?

If they are I wish they wouldn't. Mum acts weird around him, sort of giggly and girly one minute and angry the next.

God! I've just had the weirdest thought. You don't think they'll get back together, do you? My mum and my dad? That would just be too weird.

She doesn't need to have him do everything for her anyway. I've told her Rob is more than willing to help us do up the house. He really, really wants to make a good impression, he's so lovely like that. And he's good at DIY – OK, he's not a tiler like my dad, or a plumber or anything, but he can fix stuff and make shelves and cupboards and things. He says he's going to make a crib for the baby. Mum said she'd buy us one from John Lewis but I said no. I want our baby to have Rob's crib not some posh shop-bought one. She looked at me like I was from another planet when I said this. I don't know where she gets the idea that I want loads of things buying for me – I may have been like that at one time but I was a kid then. I'm an adult now. I'm having a baby of my own.

Yesterday I saw the doctor. She was nice, didn't make me feel stupid or ignorant. She asked for dates and stuff and then told me I was six weeks' pregnant and that the baby is due at the end of February. Rob cried when I told him. He said he couldn't believe it, an actual baby in seven and a half months. Then he had to go back to work so I went to look around Mothercare. Kids' stuff is really expensive. Maybe I should get a job – will anyone employ you if you're pregnant?

Trouble is, I totally have no idea what I could do. I am absolutely not working in McDonald's. Rosie's going to work at her dad's office for the summer, lucky cow. Maybe I could work for Paul at Smart Homes. With my mum. Maybe not. I suppose the only option for me is to get a job in a café like her, but I think I'll just hang on a bit longer and see what turns up. I'm not that desperate yet.

✻ ✻ ✻

Stella

As I pull out of the services (second toilet stop – anyone would think I was nervous), and back into the flow of traffic, the sun beams at me kindly, all golden light and happiness. On a sultry summer's day like this, the last place you want to be is on one of the busiest stretches of motorway in the UK.

And the very last place you want to be is on your way to prison.

I have no more desire to visit my father than to pull out my eyes and mount them on sticks. I have clearly succumbed to the oldest and cruellest of tricks: emotional blackmail. Even now, as I exit the M25 to join the M23, I can't quite believe where I am or what I'm doing. Only days ago I protested to Bonnie that I would never see the man again, never give him so much as the time of day.

Have I lost my mind? Have I changed my mind?

I believe I have done neither – and possibly both. I never said it was uncomplicated.

After three and a half hours' driving, I'm edgy and red-eyed when I arrive. I am also an hour early. My visit isn't supposed to be until two o'clock, and I don't think it's the kind of place where they let you sit and have a cup of tea while you wait. Pulling into the vast car park I wonder how to pass the time without winding myself up into a frenzy. Jeremy Vine is on the radio, the topic of the day Fat Cat Payouts – which the masses are well and truly worked up about. Not my problem.

I root around in my bag to find my now very grubby list. The day when I will finally be able to go shopping for some of my "must haves" is drawing nearer, but lately, I've started to get the feeling that I've left out something really important, something pivotal to my future happiness. I unfold the sheet of paper and spread it carefully across the steering wheel.

CAN'T LIVE WITHOUT
American double-door ice-maker fridge-freezer
Kenwood food mixer
Cath Kidston Kitchenalia
Furniture! (Sofa, dining table, chairs, beds,
  wardrobes…)
Clothes: see sub-list
TV
Lipsy - computer, Playstation, iPod, clothes…
Carpets for entire house
New bathroom suite and towels ✓
Tiling - bathroom and kitchen
Bed linen x 4 - Marks & Spencer

Hmm. Immediately it strikes me that it isn't much of a list at all. Bits of it read more like a letter to Father Christmas from some gadget-deprived wannabe. Maybe the problem is that there are just so many things I can't live without that it would be impossible to get them all onto one piece of paper. My list is bound to be woefully inadequate, isn't it? Whose stupid idea was this?

At least I can now put a tick against tiling, thanks to my strangely-attentive-all-of-sudden ex. And I might as well cross out Lipsy's entry, seeing as how she's gone all anti-materialistic on me. Well, I guess she's got more important things to worry about.

Just before two I lock my car and walk across to the visitors' centre. In the brilliant sunshine, the rows of pale brick buildings look less like a prison and more like a sprawling college campus. My mouth is dry and my palms are sweaty – not just from the heat. I have no idea what to expect, or how I will be feeling an hour from now. What will he say to me? Will he be angry with me?

This last thought stops me in my tracks. That *he* may be upset with *me* had not occurred to me until now, but suddenly I picture myself in his shoes and see the situation through his eyes for the first time.

A daughter who abandoned him in his hour of need, spurning all attempts at contact for nearly two years.

Or perhaps he will be remorseful and worn down by the sheer weight of his guilt, shouldering it like a brickie's hod, searching for a place to let it rest…

For God's sake! Why am I doing this to myself? I shake off the image of my father as a saddened, wizened, crestfallen figure and replace it with one of him standing defiantly in the dock, like the last time I saw him. If I am going to do this, for Lipsy and for my mother, I need to be strong. And I've always found my best reserves of strength come from that place, deep inside, where I'm permanently angry. With a final deep breath, I square my shoulders, lift my chin and enter the prison.

Chapter 16

Stella

I needn't have worried about a detrimental change in my father's physical appearance. The man I instantly recognise is as healthy and hearty as ever – perhaps more so. His hair is still clippered down to a number one all over, a vanity he acquired when he realised he was going bald. His colour is good, and I notice that his shoulders seem wider than before. Has he, veteran criticiser of gyms, been working out?

I had pictured the inmates dressed in some kind of degradingly banal overalls – a bright orange or yellow maybe, a bit like my uniform at Café Crème. Instead, my father is wearing jeans and a pale blue shirt, not unlike the kind of clothes he'd worn on Sunday afternoons when we were kids, when he would potter about the house doing this job or that, chasing us with a hammer and a comedy, fake-horror expression on his face.

OK. I need to stop these thoughts now.

He rises when he sees me, and the look of sheer pleasure mixed with astonishment on his face nearly finishes me off for good. I keep my cool and sit across the table from him, smoothing my new gipsy skirt underneath me and taking a long time to adjust my bag on the floor by my feet.

He waits, watching me the whole time.

With as much ice as I can muster, I say hello.

'Hello, Stella.'

Where my voice was all frost and hardness, his is deep and mellow, and in those two words he manages to convey a gratitude I'm not sure I understand.

'So. This is prison then?' I glance around, mainly to avoid his intense stare, and instead I catch the eye of the guard who checked my holdall when I came in. He winks at me salaciously. Bloody cheek! I jerk my head back towards my father and make my expression challenging. 'Bit of a holiday camp, isn't it?'

My father smiles and reaches across the table for my hand. 'It's so good to see you, Stella. I've missed you.'

I snatch my hand away as though his touch is acid. 'Well, you've only got yourself to blame. If it wasn't for your greed we'd all have been better off and you wouldn't have to miss any of us.'

Already I've given away more than I wanted to. So much for being cool. I remind myself that I'm here to do the decent thing and that all I have to do is go through the motions and soon it will be over.

'How are you?' He asks this almost casually, as if he's been away on holiday or something.

'Oh, I'm fine. You know, having lots of fun, going to lots of places with interesting people, the usual stuff. And you?'

The smile is starting to slide off his face now and I wonder what the hell he expected. After all this time did he think I'd just waltz in here and all would be well? Does he not realise how angry I am with him for deserting us like that?

He takes a moment to readjust then speaks again. 'I heard about your house. I'm so sorry.'

'Why are you sorry? That, at least, wasn't your fault.' Although in some ways maybe it was…

He ignores me and carries on. 'It must have been a terrible shock, waking up one morning and finding that. I can't imagine. Billy tells me you didn't have any insurance. It is a shame but I do understand, Stella. I know how difficult it can be to keep a track of these things.'

144

I don't know if it is the sharp reminder that he and my brother have had a relationship all this time from which I've been excluded (the fact they had been discussing me only makes it worse), or the audacity of him comparing my small housekeeping difficulties with his enormous – and illegal – financial misdealing.

Whatever it is, I suddenly feel sure that if I stay for one more minute I will have to hit him.

I stand up, scraping my chair across the floor and making the woman just across from me wince.

'This was a mistake,' I hiss, and snatch up my bag. This time his hand tries to grab hold of my arm, but I shake it off violently. One of the guards calls out. I don't hear what he says, but my dad drops his hand and pleads with me in a low voice.

'Stella, don't go. Please. I know it's hard, I really do, but you've come all this way. At least give it a chance. There must be things you want to say to me, stuff you need to get off your chest. I want to listen. I do. And I … There's something I need to tell you too.'

Well, of course, that gets me interested. I make a point of standing for another minute though, hoping it will at least embarrass him in front of the other inmates, and then I sit down primly, folding my hands safely in front of me.

'Go on then,' I say, 'let's hear it.'

Now he seems reluctant to speak. Maybe it was just a ruse to keep me here.

'You have something to tell me?' I prompt.

'Yes, I have.' My father leans back, crisis temporarily averted. I'm still on the edge of my seat though. I could bolt at any minute. 'But first I'd like you to tell me why you haven't been to see me before now.'

'Are you crazy? You really need me to spell it out for you?'

He nods, his face grave. 'I think I must do. At least, I need to hear it in your own words. I've sent you visiting orders

145

before and I've sent you letters and messages via your mum and Billy. I wanted you to hear my side of it, there never seemed to be time before the trial –'

'You were too busy selling off the family assets to save your own skin.'

'I can see that it looked that way to you. And I can see how angry you are. So you do blame me for everything? For all of it? Without ever giving me a chance to explain?'

I look into his eyes and see that he is genuinely puzzled by this. Time to put him in the picture.

'Do you know what life has been like for us since you were put in here? For me? For Mum? Do you even care? My mother – your wife – has virtually no money to live off and has the spending habits of Posh Spice. She buys more useless tat than even she knows what to do with and has been running up credit card bills faster than you can say "balance transfer". How do you think she's paying for the mortgage and the gas bill, not to mention the satellite TV subscription and the bloody membership for a golf club she never goes to anymore?'

I lean forward. 'Go on, *Dad*, tell me. Because you've obviously given it a lot of thought while you've been locked up in here. I mean, you haven't just pushed it out of your mind and hoped it would all go away, have you? Not my wonderful, responsible father.'

At this, my not-so-wonderful, not-so-responsible father puts his head in his hands and, to my horror, starts to cry. His tears are silent, more of the wracking kind, but even so, I begin to fear for his safety. I mean, he's in prison. Where they beat you up for being weak. Or worse.

'Dad,' I say quietly. 'Dad, come on. Stop it now. You don't want that lot to see you like this.' My sweeping nod takes in the guards as well as the other inmates. This may be an open prison, low security and all that, but they look a pretty rough bunch to me.

'Stella.' My father clutches my hand again. This time I let

146

him. 'I'm so sorry for what I've put you all through. I had no idea. I really didn't. Billy and your mum, they never said anything... I'm so sorry.' Oh God, he's off again. Honestly, how has the man survived in here? I'd forgotten how emotional he can be. Come to think of it, it was a bit of a family joke when I was a kid, how "real" men are those who can show their feelings, not hide them. I just wish he'd repress them a bit right now.

'OK,' I tell him, patting his hand tentatively. 'It's OK. There's nothing anyone can do about it now, is there? You didn't mean for it to end up like this, I guess.'

Listen to yourself, making excuses for him. But I've never been good around people who are upset – that's why I avoid my mum; she's always upset about something. If she's been coming to see him regularly, and she obviously has, it's not surprising she's been in bits about it.

'I'm so sorry,' he says again, and I shake my head, trying hard to hold back my tears.

We sit in silence for a while. Other visitors are starting to leave now, hugs exchanged, tears shed. A small child clings onto his mother's leg shyly as she pushes him forward towards a frighteningly emaciated man. Who would bring their kid to a place like this?

I reach into my holdall and pull out the bag of Murray mints I bought at the services. My dad takes them gratefully – too gratefully – and I shake away his thanks. He promises to send me another visiting order in a fortnight and I try hard not to feel too pleased. Do I want to visit him again? I'm not sure I could go through this twice.

'Dad,' I say as the room empties, 'you said you had something to tell me.'

'I do, Stella. And it's important that you believe me. Really important.' He is standing now, looking over his shoulder at the cheeky guard, gauging how much time we've got left.

'Well? What is it?'

As he starts to talk the guard looms over me and says it's

147

time to leave. I shrug him off and turn back to my dad, still holding his hand, still searching his eyes. 'Well?' I say more urgently.

My father meets my gaze, his expression steady and calm once again.

'I didn't do it, Stella. This is the truth – what I said in court was the lie. I'm innocent. Completely innocent.'

* * *

Paul

Clever Carpets was a shop with a name Paul felt perfectly justified in being suspicious of. Smart Homes had seemed the obvious choice for his own business – that his surname lent itself to such use was just lucky. But companies who chose names so obviously dubious were at best fly-by-night, or, in the worst cases, extremely dodgy.

The store, in one of Milton Keynes' many retail parks, occupied a surprisingly large amount of space and boasted, according to their advertising, "the widest choice of floor coverings you'll ever see". Hmm, really. Paul was also highly suspicious of spurious and unprovable claims. He regarded the spotty young sales rep with careful eyes, determined to step in at the first sign of dodginess.

Stella seemed happy enough, though. She'd found the advert in the local newspaper, pointing it out to Paul yesterday afternoon. He hadn't the heart to tell her that she really should be attending to the viewings diary (i.e. doing her job) and not trawling through the papers.

They'd reached a tenuous understanding since that night at the pub – or, at least, Paul had. He understood that Stella was still pretty messed up and that now the lowlife was back on the scene, Paul would have to keep his newly discovered feelings to himself. At least until things had settled down a bit. He also understood that, as they worked together and she was one of his best friends, stopping those feelings from growing even deeper was going to be nigh on impossible.

Stella was, of course, oblivious to all this. She seemed to have recovered from her embarrassment and had even joked about her clumsy pass a few times. Paul longed to tell her that it had been far from clumsy and that he wished more than anything that he'd responded in kind at the time. The one thing she had made crystal clear was that she didn't want to lose Paul as her friend and this, he told himself, was at least something.

It would have to do. It was all he had to hold on to for now.

'What do you think of this one?' She held out a sample of muddy-brown carpet, her face lit up with enthusiasm.

'It looks a bit like your old carpet does now. After the fire damage, I mean.'

Stella's face dropped and she hesitated for a moment before trotting off to find another. 'I know just what you mean,' she called over her shoulder bravely.

The old Stella would have told him to mind his own beeswax or said he had no taste anyway and why was she even asking him. This one was still too careful around him.

Paul missed the old Stella. If only he could turn back time.

'You should choose whatever you like,' he said, catching up as she continued to search through the vast swathes of samples. The sheer volume of fibre was starting to make him feel itchy. 'You're the one who'll have to live with it, not me.'

Why did she suddenly look at him so sadly? What had he said? He was only trying to be supportive. In lots of ways, Stella was just like every other woman he'd ever known – impossible to understand without a manual.

'So I went to see my dad.' Stella had her back to him and threw this comment out carelessly, out of the blue. Paul was sensitive enough to take his cue and answer in a similar casual tone.

'How was it?'

'Good. Fine.'

'That's good.'

'Yeah.' She turned to face him again and smiled. 'It was good, actually. Surprisingly so. I'd expected, oh, I don't know, for him to be defensive. He wasn't, though. In fact, he said… Well, it doesn't matter. But it was all quite normal. Considering.' Paul nodded sagely. He had no idea what passed for normal during a prison visit. 'So thanks,' she said. 'For persuading me to go.'

'Did I?' Last Friday's conversation had taken such an unwelcome turn that he hardly remembered this part of it, but he wasn't going to bring that up now.

'You did, yes. So thanks.'

Stella seemed to be wandering aimlessly amongst the racks of carpets so Paul guided her to a section marked "100% Wool", mainly to avoid being accosted by the aforementioned spotty youth who was making a beeline for them.

'I can't afford any of this,' she said, fingering an oatmeal loop wistfully.

'What was prison like?' asked Paul, genuinely interested.

'Pretty much how you'd imagine, really. I got searched going in. Nothing too invasive but, honestly, there was this guard who was very familiar. And I don't mean I thought I knew him, I mean *familiar*.'

'Was there, now?' said Paul through tight lips.

'There's a list of things you can and can't take in, and you have to queue up and wait for the visiting room to open, which is just like you see on TV, small tables with chairs either side. Not too forbidding, really.' Stella picked up another sample and, after checking the price, pressed it to her nose.

What sort of person smells carpet?

'It's an open prison, isn't it? I always thought that sounded like they can just walk out if they want to.' Paul sniffed the nearest carpet himself. Now he wanted to sneeze as well as scratch.

150

'I don't think they can, Paul. It wouldn't be prison if they could just leave, would it? Dad has a job in town, in a builders' merchants. He goes there twice a week and helps out. It's part of his rehabilitation. But I'm sure it's heavily supervised.' She went quiet after this, not even smiling at the young salesman when he appeared again out of nowhere.

'Come on.' Paul took her arm and propelled her towards the exit, which suddenly seemed to be very far away. 'Let's go and have lunch somewhere. We can do this another time.'

Stella let him guide her outside but when they were in his car she turned to him and said, 'You know, I think I'll go back in there. I have to sort this out today, you see. It's important.'

Paul couldn't see why when, as far as he knew, the house was still in need of an all-over paint job, not to mention a new ceiling in the kitchen and floorboards on the landing. He'd offered her Ray the handyman again for these jobs, and had been surprised when she'd refused. Typical Stella, he thought. Always so independent.

'I'll come back in with you,' he told her.

'No. You go. I've taken up enough of your time already.'

Taken up his time? What the hell did that mean? Wasn't that what friends did?

'Have you been to see Hannah again?' Stella asked, completely out of nowhere.

'Yes. And Sharon's agreed to let me bring her over to my flat next time. Why?' Paul tried to read her face but she was gazing off into the distance now, her eyes inaccessible. 'I thought we'd agreed not to talk about Hannah,' he added softly.

'Did we?' Stella turned back to him suddenly and he felt the full force of her stare. It was like being too close to the sun. 'Yes, I suppose we did. At least, that's what you wanted. But the subject of absent fathers has been on my mind a lot lately. I just wondered how it was all panning out for Hannah and Sharon now you're back on the scene.'

Paul thought he knew where this was going and he was

stung. 'I am nothing like John Dean, Stella, and you know it. What happened between Sharon and me is completely different.'

'You're right,' she answered. 'You're right. Let's just hope that Robert is nothing like him either, eh? Or we'll all be in a right mess.' She must have noticed the puzzled look on his face because she finally put him out of his misery. 'I need to sort the carpets out as soon as possible, Paul, because Lipsy's moved back home. That's the good news. The bad news is, she's pregnant.'

* * *

When he got back to the flat, the first thing Paul noticed was the smell. He wrinkled up his nose in annoyance. This was becoming a regular occurrence, and one he needed to stamp out as soon as possible. It wasn't that he objected to pot-smoking *per se*, he just didn't like it being smoked in his own flat by the occupier of his spare room.

Especially as he was soon to be entertaining his eight-year-old daughter here. He had big plans for that spare room.

'Hey, dude.' Billy was sprawled on the sofa. At least he'd taken his shoes off this time.

'Billy.' The word came out like ammo.

'What's up?'

Did he have to sound so much like an advert for the surfer generation? By Paul's reckoning, Stella's brother had, at twenty-nine, missed his chance to attach himself to that particular identity. Which made it an affectation. And if there was one thing Paul hated it was affectation.

He pointed first to the ashtray and then to the air in general. Words were wasted on Billy.

'Oh, yeah. Sorry man. Had a hard day.'

Hard day? Paul laughed. 'You know, mate,' he said, giving up and sitting in the space Billy had made for him on the ravaged sofa, 'I think it's about time you moved out.'

Billy wasn't too stoned to look shocked. Or hurt. He stared at Paul. 'But I thought we were having a laugh?'

'One of us is, yeah.'

Paul got up and went through to the kitchen where the washing up didn't get "done" anymore, it merely got stacked in a state of readiness. Ready for Paul to do it himself when he ran out of anything resembling a plate or a utensil.

He made a cup of coffee in a rinsed-out mug and took it to the doorway. Billy was making a valiant attempt to clear up the lounge but it really was too late.

'Now Stella and Lipsy are both back in their own home again there's no reason why you can't go home yourself, Billy,' Paul told him, sounding like a patient school teacher.

'Aw, go back to my *mother's*. What a drag.' Billy completed the role play like a petulant child. No wonder Stella got so irritated with him. But Paul didn't want him around anymore, and he damn well wasn't going to feel guilty about it. He'd done the decent thing and given the bloke a bed and a roof over his head; now it was time for him to move on.

'Suppose you want the place to yourself for when you bring my sis back here, eh?' Billy said, with a knowing wink.

Paul could have kicked himself for letting it slip that he might have feelings for Stella. Boy, had he picked the wrong person to confide in.

'That won't be happening,' said Paul, quietly.

'She dump you already?'

'No!' He took a deep breath. 'Your sister and I are just friends. And that's all either of us wants at the moment.'

'Just good friends, eh?'

'That's right.'

Billy jumped off the sofa and patted Paul on the back. 'I'm packing, mate. Don't you worry. Thanks for the room and everything but you're right. It is time for me to go. Back to mater, eh? Someone to look after me, that's alright.

'Word of advice, though.' He paused in the doorway and smiled. 'Don't give up on my sis just yet. I know she's a pain in the neck but she really likes you and, if you want my opinion, you two are made for each other.'

Chapter 17

Stella

This week I've been gratefully distracted by the endless small decisions to be made about my house. I was seriously tempted to just choose the same for everything as I had before. Change has been forced upon me, after all. It wasn't my doing (I keep telling myself this). But the opportunity for a total revamp is too good to miss. And I must have watched far too many home make-over programmes because before long I am stacking up the paint pots in creamy neutrals and light-reflecting naturals.

The experience reeks of *déjà vu*. When we first moved into this house I agonised alone over each of these decisions – curtain poles, curtains, carpets, walls, furniture. It was my first home. It meant everything to me.

And now I have to choose all over again. There is a part of me that finds it fun, but there is another part that feels incredibly guilty for neglecting my maintenance responsibilities and not having insurance, and that takes the edge right off.

Having Lipsy home is wonderful. Really wonderful. Apart from the obvious, lurking problem of a baby on the way, life with her is perfect. She is considerate and warm and polite. She cooks meals for me when I come in from work and meets me after my shifts at Café Crème so we can go for pizza together. I don't know what's happened to her: could it be that the new life inside her has caused some kind of personality shift? Whatever it is, I'm not complaining!

We even went to see a film this week. I can't tell you anything about it because I spent the entire two hours pinching myself. Is becoming a grandmother too high a price to pay for getting my perfect daughter back? I'm starting to wonder.

We're having our decorating party this afternoon. Lipsy organised it for me. She phoned round all our friends (didn't take long), roped most of the neighbours in, Joshua included, and persuaded my mother to come along to make the tea. Robert turned up an hour ago with a bag of paintbrushes and an enormous roll of plastic sheeting for the floors. I didn't have the heart to point out that as the floors are still only bare concrete it doesn't matter if they get splashed with paint. It was a nice gesture.

Yes, I am warming to him. Seeing the two of them together gives me hope, that's all I'll say. But I won't tell him that, oh no. Or Lipsy. I'm not ready to throw in the towel and support this nonsense openly. Not yet.

Bonnie is the first of our party to arrive. I'd expected her in some kind of designer overalls – Bonnie has a way of making clothes into costumes. But she's just wearing old jeans and a too-big T-shirt and looks amazing of course. Marcus has brought Cory with him.

'He can do the skirting boards,' Bonnie jokes.

The more the merrier, I say.

Pete and Louise squeeze through the door next, attached at the hip, dressed identically. Lipsy sets them to work in my bedroom, my soon-to-be "Relaxation Haven", but I wonder if this is a good idea. Newly-weds, brand new king-size bed – do I have to spell it out for you? The floaty lady from Number One, Sandra, brings a cake she baked herself and some crystals for the house's feng shui. Triffic.

Soon Number Three, Chaplin Grove is full of music and laughter and toxic paint fumes – I couldn't afford the expensive, odourless type and I'm sick of explaining that. Paul is in the lounge talking to Sandra while he slaps a load of Pacific Breeze around, and Lipsy and Rob are tackling the dining room. I'm flitting from room to room, dishing out directions and compliments in equal measure. I give Lipsy yet another hug to thank her for organising the party, and I'm thrilled when she doesn't shrug me off. To reward her I give Rob a subdued smile.

My mood is good. Buoyant, even. It is ruined a little, however, when John Dean turns up (uninvited) looking devastatingly handsome and carrying a very macho bulging toolbox. When he arrives, squeezing past me in the narrow hallway with a mischievous grin and an unmistakeable leer, I can see straight through to the kitchen – straight through to Paul. He does not look happy. He has an almost pathological hatred of John Dean.

Not my problem. I have enough to deal with as it is.

As I survey the activity going on in my little house, I'm struck by an exciting thought which makes my future self tingle with possibility. I could do this for a living. I mean, I could do up houses for a living. With help, obviously, even the kind you have to pay for. I could buy run-down, damaged or unloved houses, do them up on a budget and sell them on for a profit. I could become a Property Developer.

Now, you may laugh – after all, how many people have thought this and fallen flat on their faces? But I have the credentials. I've done it once, that's got to count for something. I've also done it on a budget of nearly zero, which makes me better at managing the money side of things than most of those wannabes on the TV. I work for an estate agent, albeit as an administrator, but I know about house prices and I also know the local area like the back of my hand. Which estates are a no-go, which are a guaranteed earner.

And, a fact not to be dismissed, my dad is a builder. A soon-to-be-available and out-of-work builder. Pictures of a father-daughter business empire form in my mind. Obviously

I would take charge of the finances – he's marked his card in that department.

Lipsy interrupts my musings with a cup of weak tea and news of an accident in the bathroom.

'Joshua's ruined the new shower screen,' she says, and I dash upstairs, daydream abandoned.

Joshua, it seems, was a little too eager in his cleaning and has scoured the protective surface off the screen. That John Dean had to be the one to point this out to him doesn't seem to have done much to improve the atmosphere.

'It was an accident,' Joshua is saying as I burst into the tiny room. 'Anyone could have done it.'

'You've rubbed the bloody thing away completely. I only installed it yesterday.' This is an exaggeration – he actually installed it three days ago, along with a new extractor fan and a bathroom cabinet to die for. He gives me a smile now and shakes his head at Joshua. 'What are you like, mate?'

At least he's not the type to rub someone's nose in their mistakes. Joshua, I'm happy to say, still has his ego intact and turns away to tell me he's very sorry.

'That's OK,' I say reassuringly. 'I'm just glad of the help. And I'm sure it wasn't your fault. The shower screen is probably one of those really cheap ones. It was only a matter of time before it happened.' I throw John Dean a withering look.

'Not if the cleaning was left to you it wouldn't, Stella,' my ex says mockingly. 'Unless you used a scouring pad on it like this muppet.'

I pull Joshua out of the bathroom before a major row erupts. Typical of my ex to try and make a fool out of any other man in the vicinity. Thank God Paul is safely occupied downstairs. 'Take no notice,' I tell Joshua. 'He's the muppet, not you.'

My neighbour goes to work on the kitchen cabinets instead, and soon he and my mother are happily discussing the merits of modern-day cleaning fluids over old-fashioned remedies. Mr Muscle versus vinegar. Stain Devil versus baking soda. I leave them to it.

'He's a nice bloke, isn't he?' Bonnie says as I walk out of the kitchen. She is gesturing towards Joshua with her dainty head.

'Yes, he is. A really good friend. Especially if you don't like housework much,' I say, laughing.

'Seriously, Stella. You could do a lot worse.'

'Oh, come on, Bonnie.' I steer her back into the relative privacy of the dining area. There is a little posse of painters gathered in the far corner of the lounge and I don't want them to overhear. 'Joshua? He's more wife material than husband material.'

'Rubbish. You're just so used to bad boys you don't recognise a good thing when you see it.'

'"Bad boys"?' I repeat incredulously. 'Who are you, my grandmother?'

'All I'm saying is, there's nothing wrong with a nice man who takes a pride in his house and likes to cook. Unless...' she lowers her voice. 'He's not *gay*, is he?'

'I've no idea. We went out on a couple of dates but then it just sort of fizzled out.' I didn't tell her that the reason it fizzled out was that I realised I was in love with my boss. 'He clearly wasn't interested in me in *that* way but I don't think that makes him gay. Lots of men aren't interested in me in that way,' I add sadly.

'Rubbish,' Bonnie says again. 'You're beautiful. And intelligent and kind and loving. Any man would be lucky to have you.'

'Thanks, Bonnie.' I'm genuinely touched.

'But you do have a tendency to miss what's right under your nose, especially where men are concerned.' If only you knew, I say to myself, thinking about Paul. 'So?' Bonnie says. 'What's the story with old flash-pants up there?'

She's never used this expression before but I instantly know who she's talking about, and the image fits John Dean

159

so perfectly I collapse into laughter, sitting on the floor while Bonnie squats conspiratorially by my side.

'There's no story,' I say when I can speak again. 'Well, there is a story but it's an old one and you already know it.'

'You can't fool me, Stella. I know sparks when I see them and I see sparks between you two. And they're not old sparks, either.'

Is she right? Are there sparks flying between John Dean and me, even after all this time? I know he still has a weird effect on me but I just put that down to old feelings which have never been properly dealt with. All that stuff I said to Paul about being confused (boy, do I regret that now!) was drunken rubbish, verbal diarrhoea. I wouldn't consider going back to John Dean in a million years. I'd have to be mad to step back into that muddy pond.

'You'd be mad to go back to him, of course,' Bonnie says, echoing my thoughts. 'But then again, people do mad things when they're in love.'

'I am not mad,' I say, a little shakily. 'And I'm not in love.'

Not with him anyway.

'No, you're not. But there are still some strong feelings around, aren't there? For both of you. Look at how he's round here all the time. He wants something, Stella. The John Dean you've told me about wouldn't be doing all this out of the goodness of his heart. Sooner or later he'll want the favour returned. And you're going to need to think about it seriously. Sooner rather than later.'

'Think about what?' I'm not dense – I just want to hear her say it.

She stands up and looks down at me. 'About whether or not having a child together is a good enough reason to give it another go. Only you know the answer to that.'

As Bonnie walks away I catch sight of Paul, opening another tub of paint, lit from behind by the sun and smiling up at Lipsy. I think about how unfair life is, how often fate gets it so wrong. Lipsy should be Paul's daughter, and the

160

three of us could have had – could be having – the most wonderful lives together.

And then I remember that Paul already has a daughter, and Bonnie's words roll around my head. Was having a child together a good enough reason to give it another go for Paul and Sharon?

Paul looks across and smiles at me, his blue eyes crinkling with laughter. I raise my hand in a mock salute and turn away before he can see the tears blurring my eyes.

***

Paul

Paul drove into Crownhill and double-parked outside Stella's house, beeping his horn lightly to get her attention. The place was looking great now, with a new front door and freshly painted windows. The decorating party had been a brilliant idea – and a great opportunity to make himself indispensable to Stella again. What he hadn't banked on was John Dean turning up, looking like an extra from DIY SOS and tackling every job that required any skills that were remotely masculine.

Which had pretty much left only the unmasculine ones, like painting and cleaning. And who had the cleaning all sown up? Joshua, of course. Not that Paul felt threatened from that quarter anymore. Not really. It was just that for such a long time *he* had been Stella's only male friend, and it was hard to see her laughing and joking with another guy, no matter how innocent or platonic it was.

No, it was definitely John Dean who was the problem. Anyone could see that he was desperate to get Stella back. Everyone except Stella. She had blithely flitted about the place all day, totally ignorant of the underhand efforts which were being employed to get in her good books.

Efforts which Paul had been a big part of, he had to

admit. Not that she'd noticed. Oh no, she was too busy being impressed by her ex's handiwork. 'Oh, John, you've made such a good job of the kitchen.' 'Oh, John, how can I ever thank you for replastering the ceiling.' OK, maybe he was exaggerating a little. Stella wasn't the type to simper. But she had seemed just a little too responsive to her ex's efforts, and not responsive enough to Paul's.

At least he'd managed to get her on her own long enough to ask her about today. Her face had lit up when he told her what he had planned; she had seemed genuinely excited about meeting Hannah. But then bloody John Dean had walked in and ruined it all. Typical.

At least he had her to himself today. He smiled and sat back, waiting for Stella to burst from her house, late and flustered as usual.

The sound of a high-pressure hose caught Paul's attention and he turned to see Stella's neighbour washing his sports car. So over the top, thought Paul. Showy. But that was Joshua all over: all show and no substance. Joshua waved, and Paul smiled through gritted teeth.

Only ten minutes late, Stella burst from her door as predicted, looking even more gorgeous than expected. She waved to Paul, a big grin on her face, and then shouted hello to Joshua. Paul gave her a lingering hug when she finally got into the car.

'What did I do to deserve that?' she said, pulling her seatbelt across her stomach and slotting it into the holder with a satisfying click.

'You're just you,' was the best Paul could come up with, feeling a bit guilty that the main motivation had been to make Joshua jealous, and trying not to focus on how the strap of the seatbelt pressed into the fabric of Stella's top and separated her breasts into two perfect mounds.

Get a grip, Smart, he told himself.

'So,' Stella was saying, fiddling with the car radio. 'Am I allowed to ask – have you sorted everything out with

Hannah's mum now? Like, does the kid know that you're her dad yet?'

'She does, yes. But I don't think I should be getting her to call me "Dad" just yet. It might confuse her.'

Stella gave him a look he couldn't interpret. 'No,' she said. 'I guess not. What is wrong with this radio? I can't find anything except voices. Where's all the music?'

'It's Radio Four. I don't think it's your cup of tea.' Paul laughed and reached into the glove compartment. 'Here, try this.' He handed her his latest purchase.

'The Kaiser Chiefs,' she read. 'Hmm, I suppose this is trendy music, is it? What the happening guys are listening to?'

'Well, yes and no. But really, Stella, the minute you use the words "trendy" and "happening" you move yourself out of that department straight away.'

'Oh I do, do I?'

Paul risked a glance across the car and saw she was smiling. He returned her smile and experienced one of those rare moments where everything seems to click into place perfectly, where all seems to be right with the world. Stella held his eyes for a moment. Then she looked down at her hands, the smile lingering around her mouth and creating dimples in her cheeks.

He drove with one hand on the gear stick, imagining her reaching out and laying her hand on his. He thought about how this day out with Hannah was a fantastic idea; show Stella what a great family guy he was and impress the hell out of his daughter at the same time. He just knew Hannah would love Stella. She had that way with kids; he'd watched her bring up Lipsy and do a great job of it so he knew what he was talking about. Until Lipsy turned fourteen, of course, but that was teenagers for you. The thought of Hannah as a teenager, stroppy and difficult, rude and sulky, filled Paul with a feeling of excited anticipation he wanted to bottle and keep.

When they arrived at Hannah's house, Paul pulled onto the drive and waited, not risking a beep of the horn this time.

After a minute or two Hannah emerged, as angelic as ever in a pink knee-length dress over white tights. What a princess, he thought, and then looked around to check he hadn't said this out loud.

'Hello, Hannah,' Paul said solemnly when his daughter reached the car, noticing her hands were wrapped tightly around a sparkly handbag. 'This is Stella – she's coming bowling with us, remember? I told you on the phone.'

Stella had got out of the car and was crouching down next to Hannah, making all the right noises, complimenting her outfit and her headband and the little bag. 'What have you got in there?' she asked, bending her head so Hannah could whisper her answer directly into her ear. 'Ah,' Stella said, standing tall again and nodding seriously. 'I always carry one of those too.' While Paul strapped Hannah into her seat, Stella caught his eye and gave him a secret wink that made his heart beat just a little bit faster.

On the way to the Xscape complex, Paul tried to join in the conversation that was flowing just out of his reach on the back seat, where Stella had insisted on sitting with Hannah. As predicted, the two of them got on like a house on fire – bad choice of metaphor, must not use that in front of Stella – and soon Paul was feeling royally left out. Not that he minded one bit. It was great to see the two of them so happy. There would be plenty of time for bonding later. Today was just about having fun. Bowling and pizza, maybe watch the skiing, to everyone else's eyes just another happy family enjoying a Saturday afternoon out. No need to make it any more complicated than that.

Chapter 18

Lipsy

Sunday 22nd July

There's a baby inside me. An actual baby. It's the weirdest thing, the weirdest feeling. According to the book grandma got me from the library it's about the size of a grape now, but on the internet when I looked it up it said it was the size of a baked bean. So I guess even the experts don't know everything. In the pictures it looks like a seahorse, a tiny little baked-bean-seahorse growing in my tummy.

Rob is getting on my nerves. I haven't told my mum this – she's only just starting to talk about him without hissing. I told Rosie but she's no use; she's been all weird since I got pregnant and I think it's because she hasn't done it yet (although she said she had before, it was her who told me it was "awesome", which it certainly is not).

Anyway, Rob is starting to act weird too, like an old man, talking about "our responsibilities" and "being sensible". I'm not allowed to drink, apparently. No one told me about that one. My mum said I'm not allowed to drink anyway because I'm only seventeen. No sympathy there.

I'm not allowed to eat Brie (which I don't like anyway but that's not the point) or pate (ditto) or rare steak (ditto with knobs on). Everyone keeps telling me to be careful, not to lift this, not to do *that, don't stretch, don't run, don't breathe! Mind you, I'm so knackered I don't feel like doing much anyway, but that's not the point. It's like I've stopped existing and all I'm here for is to provide a safe body for the seahorse.*

I think my mum has guessed how I'm feeling. Maybe she felt like this herself when she had me. She keeps trying to think of non-baby stuff to do and to talk about and I'm so grateful I just want to hug her all the time. She's been quiet tonight though, and I think she's got something on her mind. I hope it's nothing too bad; she deserves a break after everything that's happened to her recently. I think I'll get up early tomorrow and make her breakfast in bed before she goes to work. At least she won't say, 'Oh, be careful you don't fall over with that tray.' At least my mum treats me like a normal person, not an idiot.

Lipsy paused and scratched her head. It was true that her mum seemed to be the only person she could really be herself with at the moment. But her mum clearly had problems of her own, problems Lipsy would love to help with if only she knew what they were. She wondered if it could be something to do with Granddad again – her mum hadn't mentioned how the visit went but she had seemed quite upbeat afterwards. Lipsy had overheard her telling Bonnie yesterday that she might even go back and see him again on Thursday. This sounded like good news. Lipsy wanted nothing more than for her whole family to be one big happy unit – in fact she felt pretty sure she couldn't cope with the whole baby thing if they weren't.

She tapped her teeth with her pen. If her mum didn't want to tell her what was wrong there was nothing she could do about it. Maybe it was man trouble. God, she thought, what if she does decide to get back together with my dad? That, as far as Lipsy could see, would be a Very Big Mistake. Not that she didn't like him – love would be too strong a word after only knowing him a few years. But she'd picked up enough of

166

the story to know that there was a lot of history there, and not the good kind.

Besides, they just don't look right together somehow. And he clearly winds her up on purpose. Like at the decorating party, after that dippy Joshua had trashed the shower screen, her dad had followed her mum around all afternoon making digs about it.

'What's Captain Clean up to?' he kept saying. 'Where's Scourer Man?'

Her mum had tried to ignore him but eventually snapped, 'Will you just leave me alone.' She'd thrown down her paintbrush, splattering Hessian Blush all over the floor of the spare room. 'Or better still, leave us all alone. Seventeen years we hear nothing from you and now all of a sudden you're everywhere I look. You're like a virus.'

'You weren't complaining when I was doing your tiling,' Lipsy heard her dad say in what she thought was a very sulky voice. She was standing in the doorway, en route to the bathroom to carry on after Joshua had been sent elsewhere. The door was half open and Lipsy was trying hard not to spy.

'I would think,' her mum replied huffily, 'that the least we are entitled to is a bit of tiling. Not that it can make up for the years and years of maintenance payments you've missed, nor all the birthday and Christmas presents Lipsy missed out on. So you did a bit of tiling. Whoop-de-do.'

Go for it, Mum, thought Lipsy. She supposed she should feel a bit sorry for her dad, he was obviously trying his best. He was sorry that he'd been out of their lives for so long, he'd told her so. But then again, his explanation for *why* he'd been out of their lives had been a bit sketchy, and Lipsy still couldn't shake the feeling that if he didn't still have the hots for her mum (which anyone could see he did), and if he wasn't living in a dingy bedsit without a life of his own, he might not still be hanging around.

Then there was Paul. She knew he and her mum had been friends, like, forever, and he was her mum's boss and all, but

Lipsy really liked Paul; he was clever and funny and cool in a way her mum's boyfriends were almost never cool. Part of her wished that the two of them could get together. It was pretty obvious that Paul's feelings went further than just friendship. Not that her mum saw it that way.

'Don't be silly,' she'd said when Lipsy had voiced her thoughts after the decorating party. 'It's not like that at all.'

Lipsy had shaken her head and told her, 'You're wrong, Mum. I saw the way he kept looking at you today. And the way he looked at Dad. Like he wanted to punch his lights out or something.'

'Well, you might be on to something there. It's no secret that Paul doesn't like your father. But I can assure you, Paul's feelings for me do not lie in that direction. Trust me.'

'But how can you be so sure?' Lipsy had pressed.

A shadow seemed to pass over her mother's face before she answered. 'I just am,' she'd said. 'I just am.'

Lipsy wasn't convinced. 'I'm telling you, Mum, you're wrong. I *saw* him. He was looking at you like – like he was starving and you were the best dish on the menu.'

She took the pen that she'd been absently chewing (that was probably on the list of things she shouldn't put in her mouth too) and turned back to her diary. She had promised Rob she'd start a list of all the things they needed for the baby. "Clothes" she wrote and then "Nappies". What else was there to buy, really?

***

Stella

I'm getting into my car after a Sunday shift at Café Crème when the call comes through from my mother. As soon as I see her name on the display my heart sinks. We haven't talked properly since before I went to visit my dad. Even at the

168

decorating party, while she was in my kitchen playing hostess with the mostest, I was assiduously avoiding being alone with her.

What is it with my family? Why can't they just leave well alone? They got what they wanted, I went to see my dad. Was that enough for them? Oh, no. Now they want a complete rundown of how it went: How do I feel about it? How did he seem? Am I going to go again?

OK, maybe I haven't received this third degree in reality but I've had it in my imagination and that's just as bad. When my brother dropped in to see me today at the coffee shop I knew that while he appeared to want to moan about being thrown out of Paul's and having to move back home, his real motive was to pump me for information about my visit. And this was probably at my mother's instruction.

'Sod off,' I told him. And, 'It serves you right Paul kicked you out. You're a liability and I don't know why he let you stay there in the first place.' I still haven't forgiven him for running out on us all. And his excuse for not making it to the decorating party? He had a new job. Ha! That'll be the day.

I look at my phone now and consider not answering it. But, like the good daughter I would so like to be, I pick up and say a weary, 'Hi, Mum.'

All that meets my ears is sobbing and sniffing. 'Hang on,' I tell her. 'I'm on my way.'

I arrive in Shenley Church End five minutes later. It doesn't strike me as odd at first that the curtains and blinds are still shut. It's only when I let myself in the front door that I sense it. Call me melodramatic but I know something bad has happened. Maybe it's the silence. My mother hates silence; she always has the television or the radio on in the background no matter what she's doing. She even plays music low when she's sleeping. I think it's her way of drowning out the voices in her head but, hey, what do I know?

I make my way down the hall, sticking my head into the dining room and the lounge as I go. Finding no signs of life, I

169

carry on into the kitchen where I make a shocking discovery. The room is a complete mess – not so much "farmhouse" as "pigsty". This is so unlike my mother I immediately imagine the worst: kidnap, alien abduction, personality transplant.

Now I definitely know something is wrong. She is usually so house-proud she cleans all day long, except when she's shopping of course. Not in an obsessive way like Joshua: she just likes to keep it nice, she says, in case anyone comes round. Nobody ever does.

Feeling a little panicked, I climb the stairs, passing all the doors to the other bedrooms and bathroom before I arrive outside my mum's. I pause. Should I knock or go straight in? I can't remember the last time I went in there. It could be as far back as when I was a kid. I have a mental picture of pink curtains heavily patterned with roses and a kidney-shaped dressing table draped with fabric and topped with a lethal slice of glass. The dressing table was always covered with coloured bottles, boxes of powder and brushes, thick with hair.

I open the door and step inside.

The pink curtains with the roses have gone, replaced by a similar pair in cerise and white with a frilly pelmet and trim. The rest of the room is just as I remember, right down to the dressing table: they might even be the same bottles, they certainly look dusty enough. Not so house-proud in here then. Maybe she doesn't expect anyone else to see it.

My attention is drawn to the bed where I spot a mother-shaped lump underneath layers of covers. Thankfully, even from the doorway I can see that the lump is breathing.

'Mum,' I whisper, creeping over to the bed and sitting gingerly on the edge. As I sit I hear a clanking sound by my feet and I lift up a crumpled blanket to reveal an empty wine bottle and a half-empty bottle of gin (bottles of gin are never half full).

It seems I'm not the only one who's had a bad day.

'Mum,' I say a little louder.

I try to pull back the covers but she's clutching them tightly to her face. She is also crying, a faint but unmistakeable sound like the mewing of a kitten. At least she's conscious. I look down at the bottles, thinking how much worse this could have been.

I tap the lump lightly. 'Mum. What's wrong?'

Still no response. The mewing continues softly, muffled by covers. For some reason, my mother has decided to forgo the benefits of the duvet and stick with an arrangement of sheets and blankets and something she calls an eiderdown. When we were kids and our beds were made this way I suffered panic attacks when I was tucked in at night. The weight of all those layers on top of me felt suffocating.

'Mum, come on now. Come out of there and talk to me. Whatever it is, it can't be that bad.'

I pause and wait. The mewing stops, which I take as an encouraging sign. 'Something's happened to upset you and you've had a bit of a drink. It's not the end of the world. You just need some painkillers and something to eat.' My stomach rumbles right on cue. I think about the shepherd's pie sitting in my fridge and am glad I remembered to text Lipsy and tell her to eat without me. This could go on for some time.

I make myself comfortable and tell the lump that I'm not going anywhere until I find out what's going on.

'Mum, *you* phoned *me*,' I grumble. 'And now I'm here and you're hiding under the covers!'

Eventually, my mother begins to emerge. First one eye, then the other. Next, a snotty nose, followed by a mouth, blurred from crying.

'Hey!' I say cheerfully. 'And they said the Loch Ness Monster was a myth.'

She smiles feebly and sniffs. I fetch her some tissues from a box on the dressing table and make to open the curtains.

'No,' she shrieks, 'leave them closed. I look terrible.'

'It speaks!' I joke, but do as she says and leave the curtains alone.

171

While she sorts herself out I go downstairs to make a drink and find some food – I won't be a help to anyone if I starve to death. When I come back with a tray of tea and biscuits my mother is sitting up in bed and has managed to stop crying. She has also brushed her hair and blown her nose. There is a growing pile of tissues by the bed; this crying thing has clearly been going on for some time.

I pour the tea and she takes it from me with shaky hands.

'Come on then. What's happened?'

'I can't tell you, Stella. You'll be so angry.'

'Have you gone ahead and ordered that new bathroom suite?' I say, maybe a little harshly.

She shakes her head. 'No, it's nothing like that. For goodness sake, Stella, is money all you ever think about?'

Well, excuse me! The unfairness of this statement renders me momentarily speechless.

'Alistair has moved out,' she says, sniffing. 'He left yesterday. When I came back from the shops he'd packed all his stuff and just gone. No note, nothing.' She plays with her teaspoon, stirring the tea one way and then the other. She won't meet my eyes.

'But isn't that a good thing? You said I'd be angry. I don't understand – I was the one who told you to kick him out. Why would I be angry that he's gone?'

'Stella, promise you won't shout?' I nod my head mutely, although a promise like this is made to be broken. She carries on in a small voice. 'You were right about Alistair.' Well, duh! 'He hardly ever paid rent, always said he'd have it for me next week, next week. It wasn't just the last two months like I told you, it was longer than that. And he ate so much food! Never contributed to the shopping budget, even when I asked him to, which wasn't often, I admit.

'The truth is, Stella, I liked having him around. He was a good laugh and it was just company for me, that was all. Lipsy was always off with that fella of hers and you have your own life. I've got no one. Don't you think I get lonely sometimes?'

'What about your friends? Anna and Janet from up the road? All the people you used to have lunch with when you went to the gym or played golf?' I know the answer though. I only say it to mask my embarrassment.

She is right. I have never thought about the possibility she might be lonely. I would argue that it isn't my job to worry about her social life but that argument seems a bit pointless now.

'Those people stopped being my friends two years ago. I haven't gone to a gym or played golf for a long time, Stella, and you know it. You just chose not to think about it, just like you chose not to think about your father rotting away in prison all this time. Well, I have been lonely and I make no apologies for it. So what if I've been a bit of a soft touch, a bit of a mug. Alistair was a laugh, he was good company, he was …'

I grab her arm, spilling tea all over the eiderdown. 'You're not saying … please don't tell me you … with Alistair?'

'Of course not!' she shouts over the sound of my retching. 'But yes, I was a little flattered, who wouldn't be? Don't you judge me, madam.'

I have no choice but to believe her. And as the slimy toad has gone now it doesn't really matter. Her love for my dad can't be questioned. She still cries over photographs of him, still shops obsessively for that one elusive object that could give her so much pleasure it might take away the pain of missing him. I notice, possibly for the first time in my adult life, that my mother is quite beautiful: her face heart-shaped with high cheekbones, her eyes, although red and puffy from crying, still clear and expressive.

'Mum,' I say, passing her yet another tissue, 'I just don't understand why you're so upset. OK, you maybe feel like a bit of a fool, being taken for a ride and all that. And I guess this brings up some feelings, some stuff, that is quite painful.' But I don't want you to tell me about it, I nearly add. 'All that's

173

understandable. But why are you crying like your world has ended? Unless you were in love with him or something…' She howls a denial and I wave my hands to calm her. 'OK, OK. Not that. So what, Mum? What's so terrible that you're still in bed on a Sunday evening with half of Thresher's under the blanket?'

My words are met by a fresh bout of sobbing and I really am at my wit's end now.

'What is wrong with you, Mum?' I ask for the hundredth time. 'There's something else you're not telling me, isn't there? Something bad.'

My mother wails some more and I catch the words 'not worthy' and 'never forgive me'. Did she have an affair with Alistair after all? Was she behind Lipsy's pregnancy, egging her on, encouraging her? Surely not. But what the hell could it be?

'Please,' I say, stroking her hair again to calm her. 'Whatever it is, just tell me.'

She pushes me away. 'Don't be nice to me, Stella. I don't deserve that. After I tell you what I've done you won't even want to know me, let alone be nice. But…' She takes a deep breath and tries to level her voice. 'Just remember that I love you and Billy and Lipsy. And I love your father. I made a mistake, Stella. I just made a mistake.'

I'm nearly crying too now. I can't stand it any longer.

When it finally comes out, it comes in one long sentence, unprepared and unprepared for. My mother takes my hand and says, in a flat voice I hardly recognise, 'I had an affair … your father's accountant … he stole the money, not your dad … and your dad forgave me and kept it to himself to protect us all.' She pauses and looks away from my horrified expression. 'It was all my fault, Stella, not your dad's. I'm the reason he's in prison.'

Chapter 19

Stella

Two weeks after my first visit I'm back in prison. "Just visiting" as they say in Monopoly.

This time my father looks even more unsure of himself. Maybe he's been wondering if I'll turn up at all – maybe he half-hoped I wouldn't after the grilling I gave him last time.

To put his mind at rest I immediately hug him, and he looks shocked and pleased in equal measure. We sit and I hold his hand, and we talk about everything and nothing, with no breaks and no awkward silences. I tell him about the house, about my idea for renovating properties. I tell him about Café Crème and how hard I'm working to make up for my mistakes.

And I tell him about Lipsy; how I'm supporting her decision and how proud I am of how she's handling it all. My dad stares at me throughout with a stunned expression on his face, then he shakes his head and tells me he is proud of me too. I am a chip off the old block, he says. A month ago this would have sent me apoplectic; now it feels like the best compliment I've ever had.

What my mum confessed to me has, for some reason, set me free. Free to have my father back, free to show my true feelings and free to let him into my life again.

I've missed him. I don't think I realised how much until now.

I tell him about Paul, about my newly discovered feelings and the fact that I ruined it by making a clumsy, ill-timed pass at him. I gloss over the reappearance of John Dean, stressing only that it's good for Lipsy to have him back in her life. My father's face darkens at the mention of my ex, but he listens carefully and then reaches over to smooth a piece of my hair out of my face.

'You are so beautiful, Stella.'

I immediately burst into tears. He looks up at the guard who nods grimly, giving my father permission to lean across the table and hold me in his arms while I sob.

When I finally look up I see that his eyes are red, but I'm glad he's managing to hold it together. It really scared me last time when he let his emotions run wild and I've worried about him ever since.

'Has it been terrible for you in here, Dad?' I ask, blowing my nose noisily on a screwed-up tissue.

He thinks about it before answering. 'Not really. It was bad at first but then they moved me here and this place is OK. I haven't been beaten up or anything, if that's what you're thinking.'

It was and I nod, relieved.

'The worst thing,' he says, 'was being away from your mother and you and Billy. And Lipsy. All of you. That's what's been terrible, Stella, missing out on so much. And knowing that you hated me, thought the worst of me.'

'I didn't hate you,' I cry. And I wish to God that it was true.

'Yes, you did,' he says kindly. 'With good reason. I should have told you the truth. I should have trusted you. I take it you know the whole truth now? You've spoken to your mother?'

I nod, not trusting myself to speak.

'She was the one who wanted to tell you; she said she couldn't live with it any longer. We both want a fresh start when I get out of here. You mustn't be too hard on her, Stella, she had her reasons. I wasn't perfect, and God knows I gave her enough cause to be unfaithful. It was wrong and she's sorry, and I forgave her a long time ago. There's no point in punishing her now. She's suffered enough, don't you think?'

I'm not entirely sure but I nod again. 'How often does she visit you?'

'As often as she can. She always has, right from the start. She's stuck by me.'

Is he saying I haven't? I push the thought away. 'Does Billy come too?'

'Yes. Not as regularly as your mum but he does come. And he writes. Often. Didn't you know? I suppose they didn't want to tell you because you were so angry with me and they didn't want you to feel betrayed. Your family love you very much.'

'You're not the only one who's missed out for two years.' I smile weakly and my dad's face creases into a grin.

'No, I guess I'm not am I? Did I bring you up to be so stubborn?'

'Yes. And to be loyal. I'll never let you down again, Dad. I promise.'

'Ah, Stella. My Stella.' He reaches over again to touch my cheek. 'You haven't let me down. You mustn't think like that. The past is the past and now it's just that, OK? Passed.'

I smile and nod, putting my hand over his hand on my face.

We talk about the trial, about what he wishes he could change and the lessons he's learned. 'I was to blame for what happened in many ways,' he says, scraping his fingers through non-existent hair, a gesture so familiar it makes my heart hurt. 'I was so intent on making money and building this huge business empire that I didn't pay attention to what was going on around me. In more ways than one.'

'But you didn't do it, did you? You weren't laundering money. You weren't corrupt.' Or any of the other things they'd called him at the trial.

'No. I wasn't. Just incredibly stupid and naive. And greedy.'

'Then why did you plead guilty?' This is something I still don't understand. 'You let everyone think you were a bad person, Dad. You even let me think it. Didn't I deserve the truth?'

'I was trying to protect you all from the scandal.'

I laugh and he says, 'I know, I know. There was quite a scandal anyway, wasn't there? But I still think it would have been worse if it had come out about the affair. With my bloody accountant of all people. Gerald had done a bunk by the time the Inland Revenue were called in. He did a good job of covering his tracks and implicating me – he was a clever little shit, I'll give him that.' My dad runs his hands over his scalp again. 'I'm not sure why I pleaded guilty in the end. Maybe there seemed no other way. Maybe I wanted to be punished. For letting you all down. Does that make any sense to you, Stella?'

I tell him it does and we hold hands quietly, just thinking.

'Will you come again in a fortnight?' he asks me.

'You just try and stop me,' I say. 'Although, I think I'll come with the others next time if it's all the same to you. This journey is a nightmare!'

'Stella!' He calls after me as I make my way to the door with the other visitors. I rush back to his table, thinking he needs one more hug. I know I do.

'I just wanted to ask you something.' He takes my hands in his again and looks into my eyes. He's handsome, my dad, and I'm proud of him, is what I'm thinking at this precise moment. 'When I get out of here, which won't be long now, I was wondering…'

'Yes,' I prompt with a squeeze of my hand.

'Would you like me to help you with your property developing? I might be a bit of use along the way, if you could bear it. How would you feel about having your old dad as a business partner?'

178

I'm smiling from ear to ear but he hasn't noticed yet.

'I mean,' he says shyly, 'do you think you could trust me, Stella?'

The only answer I can think of is yet more hugs. I just hope he understands that this means Yes in every sense of the word.

* * *

Paul

'If you have the Beige Wool it will go with anything.'

Late Friday morning and Paul was listening to Susan's rather conservative views on carpets. Stella had brought in some samples from Clever Carpets and was struggling over which shade to choose.

'Mocha Loop is best. It will be more hard-wearing for your stairs and your hallway. That's what we went for in our house,' Loretta said without looking up.

Paul peeked out of his office, smiling to himself as Stella rolled her eyes. He knew she would be discarding Mocha Loop immediately as a matter of principle.

'You wanna get laminated, Stella. That's the way to go these days. Everybody's doin it.'

'Yes, thanks Joe,' Stella said patiently. 'But I think I would prefer carpets in the bedrooms and the lounge. For comfort, you know?'

Joe shrugged and returned to his magazine. There was a picture of a six-packed man on the front cover.

'Good magazine, Joe?' Paul called from behind his screen of filing cabinets.

'It's *Men's Health*,' Joe said, perhaps a little defensively, craning his neck to look over at his boss. 'And I am on a break.'

'Oh, OK.' Paul smiled to himself and winked at Stella, who rolled her eyes again.

179

Susan had been studying the carpet samples as though they held the secrets of the universe. She looked up with wide eyes and said, 'You are just so lucky, Stella. To be able to have any of these carpets, any one you like. And you're getting a brand new kitchen and fitted wardrobes too. I would give anything to be able to do that. To have everything new.'

Stella stared at her incredulously. Paul braced himself.

'Yeah, you're right,' she said. 'And I had to choose a new bathroom suite, and furniture and clothes and everything. Because all the stuff I had before was destroyed, Susan. In a fire. Have you forgotten that?'

'Oh, no!' Susan gasped. 'Of course not. It must have been terrible. But, you know, to get everything new is pretty cool. Isn't it?'

Paul watched Stella closely, ready to step in if an argument blew up. But she took it in her stride, shrugging at Susan and smiling benignly. Paul knew what she was thinking – that it would have been pretty cool in a way, if she'd had insurance and could afford to replace everything without having to work two jobs and break the bank to do so. He wished he could help out more. Maybe he could arrange to give Stella a bonus. He'd have to do it without the others knowing. Or maybe he could go round at the weekend and see if there were any more jobs that needed doing. That was if the infernal John Dean didn't get there first.

'Yes, it is very convenient that a confirmed spendaholic should end up in this position, isn't it?'

Time to intervene. Stella wasn't likely to let that one go.

'Loretta, have you got the details on the Campbell Heights apartment?' Paul said, jumping up and walking over to her desk.

Loretta gave him a sugary smile and bent low to search through her desk drawer, giving him a view he would rather have avoided.

Stella was munching biscuits thoughtfully, gazing at the back of Loretta's head. *Are you OK?* Paul mouthed but she

180

didn't see him. He could see her mind was elsewhere and thought the chances of her getting much work done today were slim. He wondered if she was still digesting Loretta's comment, if it had struck too close to home. After all, she would have to admit that before the fire she had been pretty obsessed with shopping.

He wondered whether the fire had changed her outlook or whether she'd go back to her old habits as soon as she was back on her feet again. As he watched her watching Loretta he found himself hoping she wouldn't. Paul thought he liked the new Stella even more than the old one.

Who was he kidding? He more than liked her. And it wasn't getting any easier, working by her side every day.

Loretta found the piece of paper she was after and handed it to him, grazing his hand with her fingers in a gesture he found odd, if not actually inappropriate. He looked down and she smiled disarmingly.

He retreated to his cubbyhole and tried to think about something other than Stella.

Meanwhile, the office chatter turned to the subject of property prices. Paul loved to listen from behind his screen; his staff seemed to forget he was there if they couldn't see him right under their noses. Joe was harking on about all the new houses being built in the west of the city, and how he thought they were lowering the value of Milton Keynes' housing stock.

'There's just more supply than demand,' he said ominously. 'And we all know what that means.'

'What?' asked Susan.

'It means,' Joe explained patiently, 'that it's the wrong way around for prices to go up.'

Joe carried on talking about population explosion, and then Paul heard Loretta butt in.

'It's always been that way here, it's just how it is. We live in a new city. It's expanding all the time. There's no need to feel threatened by it.'

'What do you think, Stella?' Joe asked.

181

'Don't ask her!' Loretta exclaimed. 'What she knows about property prices you could write on the back of a postage stamp. I mean, she lives in *Crownhill*, for goodness sake. Where all the roads are named after dead people.' The others laughed. It was a harmless enough jibe, but Paul was already on his feet again.

'Why don't you come here and say that?' Stella was on her feet too, squaring up to Loretta in a very threatening way. Paul stepped neatly between them.

'Lunchtime,' he told Stella. Picking up her holdall he guided her towards the door. Do not pass Go, do not collect £200. Straight out of the door and into the relative peace and quiet of Midsummer Boulevard.

'I'm not hungry,' she said sulkily.

'Well I am and I'm not eating my sandwiches while you two are at each other's throats. Come on,' he placed his arm around her shoulders. 'My treat.'

Stella allowed him to lead her up the hill to the shopping centre and into an upmarket sandwich place with seating outside. She shrugged her choices and refused to speak to him until nothing was left of lunch except a few wrappers and some strips of soggy lettuce.

Paul sipped his coffee and smiled ruefully at Stella. 'If you don't mind my saying so, you seem a bit tense.'

'You've noticed.' Her own smile was not as bright as his but it was a start.

At least it wasn't him she was annoyed at. Her eyes were sad. Big and beautiful and sad. He decided to delve a little deeper. 'Do you want to talk about it?'

'Not really,' she said with a sigh. 'Let's talk about you. How are things going with Hannah?' She smiled, her eyes lighting up. 'I enjoyed our day out together. She's a great kid.'

'Yeah, she is, isn't she?' Paul felt his face moulding itself into a dopey grin.

Stella's smile drooped a little. 'I feel just terrible about the things I said. Making you doubt she was yours and all. It was unforgivable.'

'No,' Paul said, emphatically. 'You were just watching out for me. And besides, there was never any doubt about it. I know she's mine. Sharon proved that pretty conclusively.'

'You're going to make a great dad,' Stella told him, placing her hand over his and stroking his fingers with her thumb. 'She's a very lucky girl.'

Paul held his breath. There was something about the way she was touching him, about the way she was looking at him, that told him something had changed. What, he didn't know. But something was different than it had been the last time they were together. And this time Paul wasn't going to blow it.

'It's very nice of you to say so,' he replied, his voice low and husky.

Stella raised her eyes to his and he held them, trying to convey a heart full of feeling with just a look. She smiled again, her lips wide and full. Paul leaned forward, across the table, holding her hand so she couldn't pull away. He lowered his eyes to her mouth, imagining his lips on hers, remembering how good it had felt that day when she had kissed him, how incredibly exciting.

Whether that precise memory occurred to Stella at the same time, Paul didn't know, but something made her pause, stop her slow movement towards him, and lean back quickly. Maybe she feared another rejection. Paul sighed with frustration, wishing he could think of a way to tell her that he was sorry for how he'd reacted before, and that he wanted her more now than she could ever know. But the words – the right words – wouldn't come.

She cleared her throat and smiled at him a little sheepishly. 'I guess we should get back to work. They'll be wondering where we've got to.'

'Let them,' Paul said quickly. Too quickly. Stella looked at him quizzically.

'Are you in the mood for playing hooky, Mr Smart?' she asked, a mischievous smile replacing the sheepish one.

'I might be,' he answered, back on safe ground now. This kind of flirting he knew how to do; he'd always assumed it meant nothing. Now he knew otherwise. 'But only if I had a beautiful woman to play with,' he added.

Stella's eyes widened. 'Really? And where would you find one of those at short notice?'

'Oh, I don't think I'd have to look very far.'

'No?'

'No.' Paul leaned back and regarded Stella with hungry eyes. 'No, I don't think I'd need to look very far at all.'

Chapter 20

Lipsy

*F*riday 27*th* July

Today I am eight weeks pregnant. I've worked it out in my diary and it seems that the baby was conceived the weekend of the fire. I wonder if my mum has come to the same conclusion. I wonder if she blames me for bringing my dad back into her life because of all this.

Things don't seem to have got any better between them. I heard them arguing again the other night. She's like one of those moths you see at night, attracted to the light and then burned by it. I think she still has feelings for him but she's angry and scared and doesn't know what to do. I wish I could help her but I can't even sort out my own feelings right now.

Rob and I argued as well tonight. All I did was tell him that I was worried about the future – a normal reaction you might think in a seventeen-year-old pregnant person. Maybe my mum was right, maybe he is too old for me. Not in actual years but in the head. He can't seem to get into my world at all these days. Sometimes I wonder what we used to talk about before this happened. I look back at my diary and can't believe I am the same person who thought that one day she'd be famous and have it published. What a joke!

He asked me if I love him. I do, but for some reason I wouldn't *tell him. I wanted to make him see that it's about more than just love. I mean, he's being brilliant about everything, he's trying to sort out a flat for us and he's been for promotion at work. He's doing all the right things but I feel as though he's living in a dream world. I can't see how it's going to work. How are we going to afford to live together and bring up a baby? I've finished school officially now but I can't get a job, can I? What would be the point when I'd be leaving in a few months to have a baby? 'We'll manage' he says. Will we? I'm not so sure.*

Lipsy stopped writing and rubbed her wrist. Those last few words were written with such force she'd nearly gone through the paper. She had read somewhere that it didn't do the baby any good to get stressed or worked up. Lipsy had laughed at this – how was she supposed to not get worked up? Her boyfriend was driving her crazy, her mother was still mental however much she loved her, and her home was a half-decorated shell with hardly any furniture. She had a baby inside her that she felt no connection with at all and absolutely no future ahead of her other than one filled with nappies and baby sick and poverty.

A car drew up outside and Lipsy went to the window to look. She recognised the car as Paul's and she could see him and her mum inside. Not like her mum to work so late. It was half eight. Lipsy had told her mum she'd be out all night with Rob – they were supposed to be flat hunting, an activity cut short by the argument that had sprung up out of nowhere. She was glad to have her mum home now. They could curl up together in bed and eat toast like in the old days. The good old days.

She was taking a bloody long time to come in though. Lipsy went back to the window to see what the hold-up was. She couldn't see inside the car but she could see that her mum was still there. They were probably just talking. Or maybe not. Seems like she'd been right about Paul after all.

186

Stella

As if our family hasn't been through enough lately, my mum has decided to host a barbeque. This will be the first family event since Dad went into prison, so I suppose it's quite brave of her. Maybe she found her confession cathartic and sees this as a chance to have a fresh start. Lipsy says we need to bond again as a family – I just know she's been reading those baby books again. Whatever the reason, it's happening today, and I can't think of a good enough excuse to get out of it.

I spend quite a long time choosing my outfit. This is mainly because Paul will be there – OK, it's *only* because Paul will be there. After our impromptu lunch date the other day I've been feeling a lot more positive about things on that front. Maybe Lipsy was right – maybe he does have feelings for me that go beyond friendship. Maybe he just didn't realise it until after I'd thrown myself at him. Maybe – maybe, maybe, maybe.

All these maybes are getting me nowhere, but I can't deny that something feels different between us. And I can't deny that because of it I feel on top of the world.

It is a hot day, cloudless and still, the perfect opportunity to wear the floaty white dress I picked up from Monsoon in the sale a few weeks ago. It wouldn't stand up to any kind of breeze, or at least my thighs wouldn't, but hopefully I'll be safe enough on a day like today.

I take more time than usual with my make-up, and I wash and straighten my unruly hair, much to Lipsy's approval, with the result that when I turn up at my mother's everyone looks at me as though I'm the surprise guest.

Especially Paul.

I'm gratified to see the look on his face and waste no time at all sidling up to him and letting him get me a drink. Oh, all that game playing is for you younger girls. I don't have time for all that.

'You look amazing,' he murmurs in my ear as he passes me a very large, very cold glass of white.

'Thank you,' I say. 'So do you.'

And he does. Dark jeans and a white shirt – such a delicious combination on a man. Especially when that man is Paul Smart. My Paul, as I'm starting to think of him now.

We stand close to each other, not talking, just watching everyone else. I love his smell, spicy and clean. Something that happened at school comes back to me, something I haven't thought about in years. There was more of an edge to Paul back then. It was probably just him trying to be cool – I certainly fell for it if it was an act. I never knew if he would be smiling or scowling when I caught his eye on the school bus, or later in the dining hall as I queued for my serving of nameless grey stew. And boy, did I try hard to catch his eye. The lengths I went to on one particular occasion come back to haunt me now.

I was nearing the end of my third year at Leongate High. Every morning I would wake up with the same feeling of dread: when the summer holidays started I wouldn't see Paul Smart for six whole weeks. Six impossibly painful, lonely weeks during which, I believed, he would meet some incredibly beautiful woman and be lost to me forever. I absolutely had to make him notice me as more than just a sweet third-former.

And the best way to do this?

To have my hair permed of course.

I had long hair back then, like I have now, but it was cut without layers and with a great big fringe. Basically, it was the same hairstyle I'd had since the age of five and I figured the time had come to ring the changes. I was a big fan of the film *Grease*. And my favourite part – everybody's favourite part, I'm sure – was the bit at the end where Sandy has a total make-over and Danny – cool, leather-clad bad boy – falls

188

adoringly at her feet.

That was the fantasy. The reality for me was baggy-arsed black jeans (I got a detention for wearing them, Leongate having a crack-down on school uniforms that term), heels borrowed from my mother that I couldn't stand up in let alone walk in, and frizzy electric-shock hair that looked as though it had been permed on chopsticks, not the extra-large extra-soft rollers I'd asked for. I looked like a cross-dressing Crystal Tips but, with the innocence of the very-young-and-in-love, I didn't know it.

Until someone told me. That someone was Paul's best friend, and the rest of the school – or at least everyone who was outside on that very hot, humid summer's day – agreed with him.

Except Paul. He was the only person who didn't laugh, or roll around on the floor, or point and giggle and then throw things at me. He punched his friend hard on the arm and hissed something in a low voice. Then he walked over and offered me a tissue from the depths of his oh-so-cool leather jacket.

This wasn't how I had hoped the moment would pan out, and I would have given anything for the object of my affection to have missed my humiliation. Still, all it did was cement my love and reconfirm my belief that Paul was Perfect with a capital P.

And look how right I was. Shame it took me another twenty-four years to fully realise that my dream had never gone away, but I guess it's never too late. Paul looks pleased, and a little embarrassed, when I reach up and give him a light kiss on the cheek. He has no idea that that kiss was earned by a kind gesture so many years ago. Maybe one day I'll tell him.

'Get a room,' someone says, and we turn around to see Bonnie and Marcus smirking at us, bottles of lager in their hands.

I give Bonnie a look and turn to say hello to Marcus. 'No Cory today?' I ask, desperate to get the focus off Paul and me.

189

'No,' he says cheerfully. 'He's with his mum.'

'You two seem cosy,' Bonnie says with a grin. Honestly, the girl doesn't know when to leave it alone.

Grabbing Paul by the arm, I say, 'Let's go and get some food before it all runs out,' and I steer him towards the ominous-looking cloud of smoke in the far corner of the garden.

I glare over my shoulder at Bonnie, who gives me a comedy thumbs up.

As the afternoon wears on I notice that Lipsy is staying protectively close to Robert as if to shield him from her family's wrath. Not that any of us feel much wrath anymore. We've all more or less accepted the situation now, and I for one have actually started to look forward to the arrival of a baby. I can't help it, I just love babies. Anyway, I figure we need some fresh blood in our family. This time next year the whole gang will be here: Mum and Dad; Lipsy, Robert and baby; me and Paul (hopefully); Billy and…

My brother is talking to a girl I've never seen before. A girlfriend? I hope so, it might be the making of him if he finally settles down. Listen to me, all grown-up and serious-sounding.

Well, I guess I should be at my age.

'Alright, sis,' he says, catching me watching him.

'Yeah,' I tell him.

I really am all right.

My mother, in an expensive-looking pink and yellow dress, gives me a quick smile that I return. I feel strangely at peace with her for once. She has invited a few of the neighbours for good measure, and I'm happy for her, glad to think she's making friends again. Maybe it will take her mind off shopping!

The first sign I have of trouble is when I feel Paul stiffen by my side – and I don't mean that in a good way. I follow his eyes and see, to my horror, John Dean talking to Lipsy and Robert, drink in hand, looking like he hasn't a care in the world and has every right to be here.

I grab my mother's arm. 'Who the hell invited him?' I hiss.

'Who?' She looks across the patio and her face freezes when she sees my ex. 'Oh, Stella. I'm so sorry. He's been doing the garden for me. I must have mentioned it to him. I didn't think.'

My ex is wearing a red shirt and faded jeans. The fact that he so clearly knows that he looks gorgeous makes him less so, somehow. Actually he looks a bit flashy. Showy and obvious. His dark hair and rugged features are too much of a cliché. I like my men more interesting, with clear expressive blue eyes and wavy blonde hair that you just can't resist running your fingers through.

I like my men like Paul.

Turning back to Paul, I can see straight away that I have made a mistake. I looked in my ex's direction for just a little too long. 'Paul–' I begin, but he interrupts me.

'It's OK, Stella.' His tone tells me it is anything but. 'I'm going to talk to Billy, see how he's getting on.' And with that, he's gone from my side. Shame, I'd just started to get used to having him there.

Discretion would tell me to avoid John Dean like the plague, but discretion doesn't have a degree in ballsing things up like I do. I stride over to where he's standing, my eyes flashing a warning that nobody else sees.

'What the hell are you doing here?' I demand as soon as he's in earshot. I hope Paul hears me but my mother's garden is rather big and the stereo's on quite loud.

'Hi, Stella. Nice to see you too,' John Dean drawls.

'We, erm, we need some more drinks,' Robert stammers, looking at his own nearly full glass as Lipsy looks at her own completely full one.

'Yes,' she agrees. 'We do. Come on, Rob.'

They leave us standing alone in the corner of the patio, and I'm not so stupid I don't realise that this does not look good. I stare at Bonnie hard, willing her to come over and rescue me, but she turns back to Marcus and my mother. I can't see Paul but I know he's there somewhere, watching to see what I do next. But what the hell can I do? If I walk away it could look as though I have something to hide, and knowing John Dean he'd probably just follow me anyway. We could end up in an even more compromising position, somewhere inside the house, say. At least here we're in full view, and surely no one could read anything into that?

Except Paul, of course.

But if I do stay and talk to my ex then doesn't that look as though I'm happy he's here? As though I'm choosing to spend my time with him and not with Paul? Oh, for goodness sake. I could kill bloody John Dean. All those years I wanted him to come back to me and then, just as I'm moving on with my life, here he is complicating things.

He knows it, too. I can see it in his eyes. He moves nearer now, too near, and says in a low voice, 'That your boss you were with?'

'He's a good friend, actually, and I am with him still.' I'm talking too loudly, I know it, but I want to be as transparent as possible.

'He looks a lot like the guy you work for.'

'Yes,' I snap. 'He's my boss as well, OK? Happy now?'

He smirks and leans even closer. 'Getting it on with the boss, eh? Not just a pretty face. But I'm guessing it's not serious.'

'Why?' Crap. Just what he wanted, to draw me in.

'Look at the way he's eyeing up that pretty blonde. The one with the girl your brother's talking to. I'd say she was more his type, wouldn't you?' He shoves his hands in his pockets and leans back against the wall of the house. 'Men tend to go for women with similar colouring to them, don't you think? Like me and you,' he adds with a wink.

Do not let him get to you, Stella. You know what he's trying to do. My brain is telling me this but my heart is panicking, and I can't help glancing over to where Paul and

Billy stand with two very attractive girls hanging onto their every word. Get over there, my brain says. Go and be with your man. What, and give him the satisfaction of knowing I'm jealous? Yes, it squeals desperately, if that's what it takes, yes!

But I stay glued to the spot, letting John Dean's hypnotic voice drone on in my ear. He's talking about Lipsy now, about how he feels about becoming a granddad, and then he moves on to some plan he has for a new business. I'm not interested. I'm watching Paul. He looks over in my direction a couple of times and I throw him happy, light-hearted smiles that are completely false; smiles he doesn't return.

Come and rescue me, I silently say. If you're so bothered that my ex is monopolising me why don't you be a man and do something about it? If you really cared you'd be over here right now, bringing me food or a drink, staking your claim. Or maybe you're not that bothered after all.

The afternoon grinds on relentlessly. Lipsy and Robert drift back over now that I'm no longer screeching at her father, bringing with them a tray of over-cooked chicken wings and some sorry-looking ribs. God knows who's manning the barbeque – a sexist word if ever there was one: manning. And it turns out to be wrong as well, as it's my mother who's cremating all the food.

'Are you OK, Mum?' my beautiful daughter asks me.

I peer at her through the fog of smoke. My baby. She's got her hand resting lightly on her stomach, a gesture I think she's unaware of. Protecting her baby. My eyes start to fill up with hot tears. Maybe it's the wine, maybe it's the stress of the last couple of months, but I'm suddenly feeling very emotional.

And where's Paul when I need him? Where's my man, my rock, my… oh, forget it. What's the point? There he is, chatting up Milton Keynes' answer to Kate Moss. And here I am, slightly drunk and leaning on my feckless ex for support. This is not how it was supposed to be.

'Mum?' Lipsy says, concerned now that I'm openly

sobbing. 'What's wrong?'

But I can't seem to get the words out. I can't tell her how much I love her and how proud I am. Or how tired I am of struggling on my own, scrabbling about for every penny to pay for the things I think we need to make us happy. Instead, I cry. It works for me.

An arm surrounds me and starts to lead me into the house. I turn to find out who it belongs to. Paul, hopefully, or at least my mother. Or, at the *very* least, Billy.

But no. The arm belongs to John Dean, as does the shoulder I'm now rubbing my face against and the hand that's veering down my back towards my bottom. And as I'm led away, the embarrassing spectre at the feast, I'm not too drunk to know that I'm being watched very closely indeed.

Chapter 21

Stella

Putting my head in a vice and squeezing it until my eyes pop out would probably hurt less than the hangover I have this morning. It is also very possibly something that Paul would like to do to me himself, judging by his expression when I turn up an hour late for work. It's unfair, I'm hardly ever late. And I work really hard when I am here, not like some I could mention (Joe, for example – oops, I mentioned him). I may have taken a very long lunch on Friday afternoon, and now have a stack of filing the size of Africa, but that was hardly my fault, was it?

'Is it fancy dress today?' says Loretta as I try to slip behind my desk unnoticed. She sneers at me and then calls out in a sing-song voice, 'Paul! Stella's decided to grace us with her presence.'

I give her a look that says, *Why are you doing this to me?* and then put on my most winning smile as my boss emerges from behind his office-divider. He does not look a happy man.

'Why are you late?'

'I'm not. I've been here all morning. I've been working so hard you haven't noticed me, is all.'

Now, there was a time when this kind of response would have had Paul in stitches, and all I would have received in the way of a reprimand was a playful punch on the arm and the order to buy him lunch.

Sadly, for reasons I still do not fully understand, those days are gone.

'If you're late again I'm going to dock your wages,' he states flatly. 'There's a lot of work to do and you'll have to stay late to make up the time.'

So much for the sexy smiles and the gazing deep into my eyes. So much for the promise to help me out as much as he can. So much for unspoken promises of unbridled passion.

Paul retreats into his enclave and I am left speechless in the middle of the office, with Loretta smirking to herself and Susan and Joe pretending to be busy, hiding their embarrassment behind serious faces. I can't believe it. Yes, I was a bit late but there is no need to ball me out in front of everyone. What kind of a friend does that?

One that isn't in too much of a rush to drag me into bed, clearly!

Humiliated, I slump across my desk, catching sight of myself in the mirrored displays as I do. Oh, great. So that's where the fancy dress comment came from. My hair is a bird's nest and my hastily applied eye make-up is already panda-like. Not the effect I was aiming for when I got up this morning.

I work solidly and steadily for three hours then, listening to my stomach and reasoning even Paul in a bad mood wouldn't expect me to miss lunch, I walk up to the shopping centre. I grab an extra sandwich for Paul and hot-foot it back to the office.

'Eat me,' I squeak, creeping up behind him and slipping the sandwich on to his desk.

I'm gratified – not to mention relieved – when he smiles just a little.

'Hello,' he says tiredly, picking up the sandwich and peeling off the wrapper. 'Thanks for this.'

'No problem,' I whisper, and then I slip back to my desk, quitting while I'm ahead, satisfied that the delicate equilibrium has been restored. For now, at least.

Sometime around five o'clock, when the office is quiet and Paul is out on a viewing, I pick up the phone and dial John Dean's number. It's a tough job but someone has to do it.

Yes, I'll admit I was tempted. Briefly. It would be stupid of me to deny it. My daughter's father is a good-looking man and you can't wipe out a history like ours overnight. But – and it's taken me a long time to realise this – sometimes things don't work out for a reason. And sometimes that reason is simply that they weren't supposed to.

When he answers the phone I ask him to meet me at Café Crème in an hour. He has made his feelings pretty clear this time. Yesterday he came right out and suggested we give it another go. I was very tipsy, so he was taking advantage just a little. The only answer I could give him was that I would think about it, which I have. For about seventeen years. Maybe I should have talked to Lipsy first, find out what she thinks: would she like to have her mother and father back together again? Should I be basing my decision on what my daughter thinks? Probably not. And I have a feeling, a pretty strong feeling, that Lipsy would tell me to do whatever made me happy. That's what I'd tell her.

So I'll sit John down, buy him a speciality latte, and tell him thanks but no thanks. It will feel fantastic. If I have the courage I'll also tell him, calmly and without bitterness, how much he hurt me, how much he hurt us both. And that although I will accept him in our daughter's life if he manages to stick around this time, I don't want him in mine anymore. Not even as a handyman. There's only room for two men in my life right now, and even though one of them is in prison and the other is barely speaking to me, I know that they both deserve my full attention from now on.

***

197

'Paul, can I have a word with you. It's quite important.'

Paul sighed and gestured for Loretta to take a seat. 'What's up?' he said, closing down his computer screen.

'Could we maybe talk somewhere a little more private?'

'Not really, Loretta. Isn't it to do with work?'

'Oh, it is, yes. In a way.' She turned and looked around the office surreptitiously. 'It's about Stella,' she hissed. 'There's something you should know.'

Oh, great, Paul thought, this is all I need.

'Well,' she carried on, 'I've noticed that you and Stella have been getting kind of close lately.'

'I don't think that's any of your–'

'Oh, no!' she said quickly. 'It's none of my business. Of course not. It's just that, well, I like to think of you as a friend as well as a boss, Paul, and as such, I think you deserve to know what's going on behind your back.'

He was interested now, he couldn't help himself. 'Go on.'

'It happened last night,' Loretta whispered. 'I had to pop to the shops after work and I went past that café where Stella works part-time now. I have been thinking that it's interfering with her work here and doesn't show much commitment to the job … but anyway, that's not the point, really.'

Get to it then, thought Paul. Please.

'So I was passing the café and I thought I might pop in as it was open late so I went up to the door but it was locked. I thought, that's weird! The lights were on in the back there and I could see people inside, sitting at a table drinking coffee. That is,' she paused for effect, 'I could see two people.'

'And?' Paul prompted, fearing what was coming next.

'It was Stella. With a man. I hate to tell you this, Paul, as I know you have feelings for her, but they looked very close.'

'How close?'

'She was holding his hand.' Loretta thought for a moment. 'And she stroked his head at one point. He seemed quite emotional. So did she, to be honest.'

'You watched them for a while?'

'Not really, no,' she said defensively. 'I just happened to be passing, just glanced in. But it was long enough to see, if you know what I mean.'

Paul thought he knew exactly what she meant. 'It's OK, Loretta. I'm not having a go at you. I just wondered if you got a good look at him.'

'Dark hair, kind of tousled, brown eyes, handsome in that rugged way some women go for.' Loretta recited the details flawlessly. 'About six foot, well built, wearing a bright blue shirt and faded jeans.' The picture she painted was one Paul could see all too clearly; he'd been looking at the man himself only two days ago. John bloody Dean.

***

Milton Keynes could be a bit depressing at night. Especially when you were driving around it aimlessly, trying to figure out what was going on in the head of the woman you were in love with. Perhaps it was the fact that there never seemed to be much traffic – a boon when you were trying to get from A to B in a hurry but creating a strangely isolated atmosphere at other times.

Paul wouldn't live anywhere else, though. He'd watched this city grow, literally, from a sprawl of random housing estates to a vibrant, desirable place to be. And from an estate agent's point of view, it was like nowhere else on earth. It was his friend, comforting him with its long, wide dual carriageways and parks and lakes around every corner.

Usually it comforted him, that was. Tonight he couldn't find the comfort anywhere: not at Willen Lake, where he went running most mornings, not from the top of the H5, with the whole of the city spread out below him like neon artwork. Not even driving past the mirrored train station; seeing his car reflected again and again usually made him at least smile. After hours of driving and thinking and driving some more, Paul turned onto the V4 and headed for Crownhill.

He'd been considering all that had happened to Stella in the last two months and he couldn't blame her for being confused.

But the one thing he couldn't get over was the sense of betrayal. After she'd brought him lunch yesterday, Paul had started to feel guilty for balling her out about being late, and about giving her the cold shoulder at the barbeque. It was hardly her fault if her mother had invited the ex, was it? It was typical of John Dean to be trying to ingratiate himself with Stella's mum by doing her garden, but that was hardly Stella's responsibility. Paul knew he'd been out of order, ignoring her like that. He'd behaved like an idiot.

Leaving the sandwich uneaten, Paul had dragged Stella into the staffroom and demanded to know if she intended to go back to her despicable ex.

Stella had been stunned. And clearly horrified. 'No,' she'd told him sincerely, 'not in a million years. Not if he was the last man on earth. Not if someone paid me a billion pounds. No. No. No.'

Then she had given him a knowing look.

'There's someone else I care about,' she'd said softly. 'Someone very special.' And Paul had felt his insides do somersaults. He loved this woman. He believed she cared for him too. If John Dean really wasn't a threat then there was nothing standing in their way...

So he'd asked her out to dinner, a proper date he thought, candlelit restaurant, sharing each other's food. But she was busy, she said. Lipsy had asked her to go shopping for maternity clothes. How could he argue with that?

And not four hours later she had been cosying up to her ex like they were the only two people in the world. The fact was, she'd lied to him. Paul needed answers and he was determined to get them.

He studied Stella's house for signs of life. There was a light on in an upstairs window but he wasn't sure if it was hers or Lipsy's. The rest of the houses in the close were in darkness, even though it was only a little after eleven o'clock. He caught some movement out of the corner of his eye and turned to get a better view. There was a woman creeping out of Joshua's house.

Not only was there a woman creeping out of Joshua's house in the middle of the night but she was also half-naked – the top half to be exact. Strategically placed hands were doing nothing to hide the fact that she was clad only in a bra and jeans. Was this a date gone horribly wrong? Paul tried not to smile.

As the woman made her way gingerly down Joshua's path Paul slumped in his seat, hoping she wouldn't see him as she passed – he didn't want to compound her embarrassment. But she didn't turn his way. Instead, she did a quick sidestep to the left and promptly ran up Stella's own, identical path. Paul strained his eyes in the darkness to see who she was. Too tall to be Bonnie. Too big to be Lipsy. It was only when she opened her front door and the light from her own recently decorated hallway spilt out into the night that he saw her face clearly. Perfectly clearly. Stella gave a last furtive glance across the close then shut her front door behind her.

Chapter 22

Lipsy

*T*uesday 31*st* July, 11.25pm

I can't believe that this tiny seahorse-baby is making me feel so crap. I hope it's not this vindictive when it grows up. I'm knackered, nobody understands how knackered. Rob keeps wanting to go here and do this or nip off there and see such and such and I keep telling him – I'm knackered, babe. It's as much as I can do to get dressed in the morning. Some days I don't even manage that!

Rob's been such a pain in the arse since the barbeque on Sunday. Just because I had a little teeny-weeny drink of lager. You'd think I'd taken a baseball bat to my stomach the way he carried on. And mum didn't help, getting leathered like that – Rob obviously thought she was some kind of alcoholic and that it runs in the family. I'm telling you – if he doesn't back off soon …

Lipsy threw her pen across the room and watched it bounce harmlessly off her new Ikea wardrobe. It seemed like every time she wrote in her diary these days she ended up working herself into a frenzy. Gone were the days when it had been a fun thing to do, a slice of a life which had felt like it was going somewhere. Now she just moaned about sickness and feeling fat and her bloody boyfriend.

Calm Blue Ocean, she recited to herself. Calm Blue Ocean. She'd seen it in a film, someone using this mantra to sooth herself. As much as she moaned about being pregnant she didn't want anything to go wrong with the baby so she knew she had to try and stay calm. Which, with her current problems, was not easy.

As if to prove her case the front door slammed, making the whole house shake. Nice one, Mum. Setting fire to it wasn't enough, now you want to demolish it. Lipsy ran to the top of the stairs in time to hear someone banging on the door. Her mother was standing in the hallway, a horrified expression on her face.

'Mum! Why are you only wearing your bra?'

Her mum glared up at her and shook her head mutely, pointing at the door and making throat-cutting gestures across her neck.

'What? Who is it?'

'Paul,' she hissed.

Lipsy slowly made her way downstairs, trying to figure out what the hell was going on.

'I thought you were going over to Joshua's?' she said when she reached the bottom, lowering her voice when her mum shushed her. 'Where's your blouse? Did Paul do that? And why's he banging on the door? Let him in.' But when Lipsy moved towards the door, her mother grabbed her arm and wrenched her back.

'Don't let him in,' she pleaded.

'Has he hurt you? If he's hurt you…'

Lots of head shaking.

'But you are avoiding him?'

Nodding now.

'Why?' Lipsy thought for a moment then clamped her hands to her head.

'Mum! For goodness sake. Please tell me you didn't come out of Joshua's dressed like that.' More nodding, some crying. 'I don't even want to know why! And Paul saw you? And now he's angry?' That much was pretty obvious from the banging and shouting outside. 'You have to let him in, Mum.

204

He's not going away. Wait there.'

Lipsy ran upstairs, huffing with the effort. She grabbed a jumper from the pile on her mum's bed and raced back down. 'Here. Put this on first. Honestly, Mum, I'm really not up to this. I am pregnant you know.'

While her mother shrugged herself into the jumper, Lipsy opened the door. Paul stood in front of her, his arm raised to strike again. He dropped it as soon as he saw Lipsy.

'God, Lipsy. I'm sorry. I didn't wake you, did I?'

This was so stupid that Lipsy almost laughed. He must have woken the whole of Crownhill by now. 'No,' she said. 'Of course not. Come in.' She moved aside to give him access to her mortified mother. Then she stood back to watch.

'Paul!' Her mum stepped forward, holding out her hands as if to ward off the inevitable. 'Paul, I can explain. It's not what you think…'

Now why, thought Lipsy, do people always say that? In soaps and films when caught in a compromising position, people always say, 'It's not what you think,' instead of just explaining what the hell it actually is. And Lipsy was at least as curious as Paul to hear the explanation of why her mother had gone out to see their neighbour fully dressed and come home two hours later minus half her clothes. This should be good.

Paul clearly had other ideas. He ploughed straight in. 'It never is, is it, Stella? It's never what it looks like with you. Can't you just come out and admit the truth? Even your own daughter doesn't know what the hell's going on.'

Don't bring me into it, thought Lipsy.

'One minute you're flirting with me, the next minute you're getting back with her dad, and the next you're having it off with your neighbour!'

My dad? Lipsy looked at her mother quizzically. Surely not. Please, God, not that.

But Paul hadn't finished yet, and so far her mother hadn't even looked up from the floor let alone had a chance to speak.

205

'I'm more than disappointed with you, Stella. I'm disgusted.'

Her mum flinched. Lipsy said, 'Hey, come on. No need for that.'

'Really?' he rounded on Lipsy, then seemed to think better of it. 'You think what you like. And you,' he turned again to her mother, 'you can do what the hell you want. You always do anyway.'

Then he was gone, the door slamming behind him, tyres squealing into the night. Lipsy crouched by her mum who was slumped in a heap on the bare floor and stroked her head, lost for words.

When her mother finally looked up she forced a smile. 'Men, eh?' she said, then she covered her face with her hands again and started to cry.

Chapter 23

Stella

This is clearly going to be a week of waking up and regretting what happened the night before. For the second time in four days I wake with a banging head and an overwhelming sense of foreboding.

This time the head is caused not by excessive alcohol but by excessive crying. No one ever tells you that crying all night will have such a detrimental effect on your health – not to mention your looks – but it does. My skull is throbbing, my eyes have swollen into slits, my face is blotchy and – horror of horrors – there are at least four freshly broken veins on my cheeks. Damn that Paul Not-So-Smart and his jumping to conclusions. If only he'd bothered to listen to my explanation.

If only he'd picked another night to spy on me.

It was all so innocent. Joshua phoned me yesterday and said he wanted to talk to me about a "business proposition". Maybe that does sound a bit ominous but this is *Joshua*, remember. He's as harmless as a money spider. So I go round there after dinner, taking with me a bottle of red wine that was left over from the decorating party. I was glad of the opportunity to see him, wanted to thank him for all his help with the house and apologise again for my ex's crappy behaviour.

I was right not to worry. Joshua had no ulterior motives: only wanted to tell me that he'd heard I was planning a dive into the world of property and could put me in touch with his brother who is some hot-shot developer in London. He also said he'd be interested in going into business with me if I was looking for a partner. He fancies himself as project manager. I have to say, I can't think of anyone more organised than Joshua and he probably would be very useful. Plus, he has the added bonus of being seriously loaded.

But I told him I'd have to discuss it with my father, who was already on board as my partner, and by the way, did he know that my father was in prison at the moment? For some reason this seemed to unsettle him. He jumped up off his immaculate white sofa in shock, jolting me and spilling red wine everywhere.

Now, any normal person would have mopped it up a bit, said never mind, and then got back to drinking the stuff. Not Joshua, the one-man cleaning machine. Before I knew it he had his entire armoury of cleaning fluids out of the cupboard, was soaking the carpet with a combination of chemicals usually used to make small bombs, and scrubbing at the sofa like it was made of gold. He also insisted on washing my blouse there and then. I protested – who wants to end up topless on a Tuesday night for no good reason? – but he wouldn't take no for an answer. He'd already removed his own stained shirt, revealing a six-pack that made my eyes go wide. Shame he so obviously wasn't interested in me. Apart from the OCD he really could have been perfect.

I banished these terrible thoughts immediately, loyal to my perfect Paul, and shed my own top, which was whisked away and in the washing machine in a flash. (The well-maintained, not about to burn his house down washing machine.) After a short, uncomfortable silence we agreed to continue the discussion another time and I left discreetly, to spare both of our blushes.

And the rest you know. You, of course, wouldn't have jumped to conclusions like my Paul did. Anyone who knows me would have thought, 'There must be some completely

208

rational and innocent explanation for this, no matter how it looks. One that doesn't involve exchanging bodily fluids with her admittedly very handsome neighbour.'

Paul Smart thought the worst of me and the way I'm feeling this morning I figure this just about sums him up. It is with a heavy heart I dial the number for Smart Homes.

Just to make matters worse, Loretta answers the phone.

'Hi,' I say, 'it's Stella.' I can actually feel her scowl. 'Is Paul there?' I ask politely.

'Yes.' This is all I get.

'Well, can I speak to him?'

'I don't think that's a good idea, Stella. Sorry.' She wasn't sorry at all, the bitch. She was loving it.

'Why?' I'm still calm.

'He seems to be in a bit of a bad mood today. You wouldn't have any idea why, would you?' There is something in her voice that tells me she knows more than she's letting on.

'No. But I think maybe you do. Is there something you'd like to get off your chest, Loretta? Oh, sorry,' I add, because I too can be a bitch sometimes, 'you haven't really got a chest to get anything off, have you?'

This gets her where it hurts. 'At least I don't go flaunting it to anything in trousers like you,' she snaps. 'Paul knows all about your little get together with another man on Monday night. Not so very clever then, were you?'

Monday night? What is she talking about?

Then I remember. Monday after work was when I met up with John Dean to tell him 'Thanks but no thanks' and 'Goodbye'. It went better than expected – he listened and took me seriously instead of making a big joke out of it. Actually, he had been quite upset. Not devastated, I couldn't hope for that much, but disappointed – hurt even. I think he'd liked the idea of getting back together with me, moving into my little house, playing happy families with me and Lipsy and the new baby.

I didn't shout or blame or pile on the guilt. He didn't

defend or plead or argue. What he did do was apologise, I like to think genuinely, for leaving me the way he did. I told him I forgave him. I'm not sure I do completely, but I know I will one day.

And that, it seems, is what Loretta saw. God knows how she presented it to Paul – not well, I imagine.

No wonder he was so ready to believe the worst of me.

'Why are you doing this?' I ask her now. I can tell she is checking the office before she answers, making sure no one can hear her.

'Because you need to learn that you can't have everything.' I can picture her face, her screwed up mouth. She hates me. I've always known this. I've just never really known why.

'That's stupid, Loretta. I know I can't. Why do you even think that way?'

'Flouncing in and out of here, day in, day out. All the blokes eating out of the palm of your hand, you loving every minute of it.' Flouncing? I'm not sure I know how to flounce. 'And Paul, you treat him like dirt, only bothering with him when you need something, using him like some stand-in boyfriend.'

'Maybe that's what it looks like to you but that's not how it–'

Ignoring me, she carries on, 'You're not good enough to lick his boots and now he sees through you completely, just like I always have.'

It's the way she's talking about Paul that gives it away. I'd thought it was just a harmless crush, but judging by the amount of venom coming my way, I'd say she more than fancies him. It seems Loretta is in love with my Paul and is willing to do anything to discredit me.

I wonder how much damage she's managed to do.

It looks like she's played a blinder this time. She's stitched me up like a kipper, as Billy would say. I can picture her sitting at her immaculate desk, rubbing her bony hands together with glee, thinking, 'He's mine, he's all mine.'

'It'll never happen, Loretta,' I say quietly.

That shuts her up. 'What won't?'

'It'll never happen. You and Paul. I know what you've done and why you've done it, but you're going to be disappointed, my friend. He's not remotely interested in you, and even if you have managed to split us up you still stand no chance. Not in a million years.'

I don't enjoy the silence. She's a dangerous lady; if I'd realised sooner I might have tried to make a friend of her instead of letting her wind me up all the time. When she finally speaks, all she says is, 'Do you want me to give him a message?'

With a sigh, I ask her to tell Paul that I'm taking the rest of the week off as holiday. I know it's short notice but my work is up to date. It won't cause any problems. And that I'm sorry. She doesn't need to know what for.

Loretta pretends she's making a note of it. I wonder how much of my message will reach Paul's ears, if any. 'Don't worry, Stella,' she says, sickly sweet. 'You won't be missed. You're completely dispensable, and we can all do quite well without you. Better, even.'

* * *

Time on my hands. Not much to do with it. A little bit of money in the bank for once but absolutely no inclination to go shopping. What's the point of filling my house with all that stuff on my list if I've got nobody to share it with? I call Bonnie, hoping she'll be free for a coffee and a chat, or just a chat – anything, I'm desperate – but she's at work and says she'll call me for a catch-up later.

To get out of the house I decide to go to the shopping centre anyway, pretending to myself that I need to look for those all-important finishing touches, in training for my new career. There are still a few jobs left at the house, like skirting boards to finish and curtains to hang, but I'm not really in the mood.

Lipsy offers to come with me but I can see she's shattered, my fault for keeping her up half the night. I feel bad about it so I ask if there's anything she'd like me to buy for her. For her or the baby. She just gives me a look, what is fast becoming a *Lipsy* look, and says, 'You can't fix everything by buying things, you know.'

Well, I knew that! I was only trying to cheer the girl up.

'See you later then,' I say despondently as I head for the door.

'Mum,' she calls and I turn my sad eyes back to her. She laughs and comes to hug me. My daughter is finally putting some weight on. It suits her. 'Don't worry,' she says. 'It'll all work out in the end.'

Now, aren't I supposed to be the one telling her that?

Once I'm up town I drift around aimlessly for a while then find myself outside Café Crème. Shame the place just makes me think of work these days. On a whim, I head inside and grab a slip of paper from Gina. I scribble a few words on it, stuff it on Tony's desk, then give Gina a quick hug and wave goodbye.

Handing in my notice was the right thing to do, I'm sure of it. I don't need the second income so desperately now, and I miss Café Crème being my safe haven.

If only all decisions were so easy to make.

Chapter 24

Paul

Paul flinched when Loretta came to see him at lunchtime. He knew it wasn't her fault, but he couldn't help associating her with what had happened the night before. The sight of Stella standing in her hallway frantically trying to cover herself up after being with another man was too upsetting. He pushed it out of his mind for the hundredth time and turned to face Loretta.

'Sorry to bother you, Paul,' she said.

'That's OK. What can I do for you?'

Loretta leaned forward conspiratorially. 'I just thought you'd like to know she's not coming in today so there's nothing to worry about.'

'Who?' he said, knowing full well who but not wanting to give Loretta the impression that they were in this together.

'Why, Stella, of course. She phoned earlier. Just said she was taking the rest of the week off. Huh!'

'Did she say anything else?'

'Nothing!' Loretta rolled her eyes dramatically. 'Not a word. No sorry, no explanation. Just leaving us all in the lurch. Well, don't you worry, Paul. We'll manage. I've already got Susan covering the rental admin and I can do the rest. Joe's got his diary organised and I'm sorting out the website. It's all under control.'

Paul moved his head from side to side. Why did he feel so

tense all of a sudden? He just wanted Loretta to go away – he wanted the whole damn office to go away and leave him alone. He needed to think. But he knew he should be grateful; his staff were coming through for him and right now he needed them to get on with it more than ever.

'Thanks, Loretta,' he said, cracking his neck alarmingly. 'You're a star.'

She grinned and leaned even closer. 'Would you like me to massage your neck for you?'

'No!' Crap, he hadn't meant to shout it like that. 'Sorry. No thank you. I'm fine. Well, I'll let you get on with running the office then. Seems you've got a lot to do.'

She murmured something and disappeared. Paul sat back and tried to imagine what might be going on in Stella's head today. He guessed she'd stayed off work because she was too embarrassed to face him, but that wasn't like her. The Stella he knew would have brazened it out, or at least had another stab at explaining.

Well, he thought, if that's the way she wants it, that's fine by me.

***

Despite his stubborn intentions, for the rest of the day, Paul jumped every time his phone rang, and was disappointed every time it wasn't her. So when he arrived home, weary and despondent, he couldn't decide immediately whether to be pleased or dismayed to see Stella's car parked outside his flat.

The car was empty. He made his way up the stairs, rehearsing what he was going to say to her. He figured he'd give her one more chance to explain and after that, if they couldn't sort it out he would give up for good. He had truly believed they were meant to be together. He'd thought they were a perfect fit. Now it seemed like the dream was more of a nightmare, and he couldn't take the stress anymore.

But when he reached the top floor he found not Stella but

214

Billy leaning against his door.

'Hi, bro,' Billy said.

'I'm not your bro.' Paul opened the door and left it open behind him. He could kick himself for getting his hopes up again.

'No, well...' Billy had followed him in and was standing awkwardly in the middle of the lounge. 'Looks nice in here. Tidy, like.'

'It's not a great time, Billy. What can I do for you?'

'Nothing, mate. I just came for the rest of my stuff. There's a stereo in your spare room and some CDs. I borrowed Stel's car,' he added unnecessarily.

'I'll leave you to get on with it then,' Paul told him, heading for the kitchen.

'I could do with a hand down the stairs, mate,' Billy called. 'If it's not too much trouble.'

Well, it bloody is actually, Paul wanted to say. Hadn't he done enough for their family? Over the sound of the kettle boiling he listened to Billy huffing and puffing as he hauled the stereo through the lounge, wincing as it crashed against something solid.

'Come on then,' he said wearily. 'I'll give you a hand.'

Together they carried the box down three flights of stairs then came back up for the rest of Billy's stuff. It was on the way back down again that Billy said, 'My sis is pretty cut up, you know.'

Paul stared at him in astonishment. 'Oh, is she? And I suppose I'm just fine, am I?'

'That's not what I'm saying, mate. I can see you're not in the best of moods, either. Don't shoot the messenger, eh?'

'Sorry.'

They lifted the last box into the boot and Billy slammed it shut. 'She told me what happened.'

'So you'll understand why I'm not a happy man, then.'

'No, I mean she told me what *really* happened, not what you *think* happened.' Billy leaned against the car. 'She's pretty upset with you. Jumping to the wrong conclusions and all that.'

Paul couldn't believe his ears. So now it was *his* fault? 'I saw what I saw. Anyone would think the worst.'

'Not necessarily. Not if they knew her like you do. I mean, how long have you two been friends? According to her, you were finally about to get it together and things were going great. But then you're off with her because she's talking to Lipsy's dad – and you can't deny that mate, I was there. And then you immediately think the worst when you catch her in what she admits was a bit of an odd situation.'

'That's big of her.' Paul leaned against the bin cupboard, trying to look nonchalant.

'The point is, you should have given her the benefit of the doubt. Is how she sees it anyway. As I said, I'm just the messenger.'

'Did she ask you to tell me this?'

'Of course not. You know how stubborn she is. As bad as you by the looks of it. But she knew I was coming here and she made a point of telling me everything. Now, you know as well as I do that things have been a bit strained between me and my sis since I went travelling. But she chose this moment to suddenly open up to me.' Billy gave Paul a knowing look. 'I'm not that flattered. You work it out.' He got into the car and wound down the window.

'Well, what did happen then?' Paul bent down to Billy's eye level. A neighbour came outside and walked across to his garage. Paul lowered his voice. 'Why was she undressed?'

'You'll have to ask her yourself, mate. Like I said…'

Paul nodded, standing up straight again. 'Yeah. You're just the messenger.'

He watched Stella's brother drive away in her beaten-up car. Whatever Billy said, it didn't change the fact that she hadn't made the effort to come and talk to him herself. Or the fact that she had met John Dean the night before and lied about where she was. If it was all so innocent why was she hiding away?

Paul shook his head. It shouldn't be up to him. If she wanted to talk to him she knew where he was but for now, he figured he was better off leaving well alone. It was about time, he decided, walking slowly back up the stairs to his flat, that he concentrated on what really mattered in his life. And right now that was his daughter. Stella would have to wait.

***

Stella

My second day of exile.

When my brother brought the car back last night I tried to pump him for information about Paul. How did he look? Was he angry? Did he seem sad? Billy just said, 'You two need your heads banging together,' and left. He sounded like our mother.

I spent the rest of the night thinking not about Paul, as I'd expected, but about Billy. About the wall that I'd put up between us and how high I'd let it grow. Was his reaction to Dad going into prison any worse than mine? I'd ignored it, shut it out, refused to visit or even to talk about it with my closest friends. Billy had gone away, taking himself out of the situation, but he'd still kept in touch with his father. Maybe that was just his way of dealing with the pain, the way being angry had been mine.

Maybe it was time to forgive him.

If he'd let me, of course.

I tried to call him this morning, figured I would invite him and my mum to dinner or something, do a proper family thing. He was out. And now I'm driving around aimlessly, wishing it was raining and dull instead of sunny and bright so that the mood of the day would match my own.

Just after lunchtime, I drive by the office thinking: If Paul's car's there I might be really brave and go in and talk to him.

217

It isn't.

So I drive by his flat instead. And bingo, there is his Audi parked in his space. With my heart in my mouth, I go around to the front entrance and press the buzzer. Nothing. I try again. Still nothing. Walk back to my car and look up at his windows. Did I just see the blinds twitch, just a little bit? I think so. I march to the door again and hold my finger on the button until it is sore.

But Paul doesn't answer. Or, by not answering I guess he is answering all too well. He doesn't want to see me or talk to me. He's clearly not interested in hearing the truth.

But I decide to give it one more go. Back in my car, I call him, first on his home phone then on his mobile. Isn't it great these days that we have so many ways of being ignored? I fling my phone onto the passenger seat and drop my head into my hands – part of me hoping that Paul is watching from his window. Maybe I should get out of the car and stand in the middle of the car park shouting at the top of my voice. That would get his attention.

Oh, what's the point? I start up the engine and jump out of my skin when my phone begins to ring all by itself.

'Paul?' I say, shoving it to my ear.

It's not Paul.

It's Robert.

'Mrs Hill?'

'No, it's not Mrs Hill,' I tell him, 'it's Miss Hill. Or Stella. Stella is fine.' Why am I saying this? Robert has never called me before so I'm thinking it's bad news before he's even started speaking. 'Is Lipsy OK?'

'Not really,' he says, his voice distant.

'Oh my God! What is it? Tell me. Where are you?' Well done, Stella. Handling things calmly as usual.

'We're at the hospital, Mrs Hill. A & E. You'd better come. Could you come straight away? Lipsy, she's – she's not – she was bleeding and now she's in a lot of pain. Please come.'

He hangs up and I sit for a second or two staring at the phone. I notice my hand is shaking. My baby's in trouble. My baby's baby is in trouble. I look up at Paul's window one last time, willing him to see me.

'Damn you, Paul Smart,' I say out loud. 'Where are you when I need you?'

Chapter 25

Stella

Lipsy has been with the doctor for an hour now and nobody will tell us a thing. My mother sits in the corner of the family room clutching her cold coffee like a talisman, while Billy paces and Robert slumps and I alternate between the three of them offering unfounded reassurance. I fetch coffees and pat hands, all the time thinking about my daughter and her tiny speck of a baby in a room somewhere nearby.

No one had even considered the possibility of a miscarriage until now. Lipsy is so healthy, so vibrant, the pregnancy normal in every way. She is very young of course, but who knew that could be dangerous? We keep asking Robert questions: Has she been doing anything energetic lately? Has she eaten anything strange? Were there any signs, anything out of the ordinary?

I read a leaflet which tells me that one in eight pregnancies ends in miscarriage before the twelfth week. I never knew that! I slide the leaflet under my chair so Robert doesn't see.

Bonnie rushes in a few minutes later. She's come straight from work, has cancelled a date with Marcus to be here, and the gesture makes me start crying again. It's good to have her with me. She's always so capable in a crisis. But as much as I love her dearly, she's no substitute for Paul. Billy says he called him but there was no answer. He left a message, he says. He's

221

sure Paul will come when he gets it.

I'm not so sure.

The minutes tick by slowly and painfully. 'Has anybody told John Dean?' I ask all of a sudden. Her dad should be here too, no matter what has happened between us.

'I called him,' says Robert. He hasn't spoken for a while and his voice is hoarse. 'On his mobile. He said he was on his way to a job in Bristol and to let him know when there was some news.'

Mum and Billy and I look at one another knowingly. So he's skipped out on her already. I shouldn't be surprised but I am. I really thought he'd changed this time. He certainly had me convinced.

Billy shakes his head. 'He's a piece of work, that one.' I couldn't agree more.

Half an hour later a nurse pops her head around the door and tells us the doctor will be in to see us shortly. She won't say anything more.

'If you could just wait a little longer...'

Doesn't she know what waiting feels like?

* * *

Just after seven, a doctor enters the family room. He stands near the doorway looking young and unsure of himself and we stare back at him as though through one eye. The doctor tells us both mother and baby are fine.

'Tired and needing a lot of rest. But fine,' he says, straining to speak above the cries of 'Thank God!' and 'Yes! Yes!'

The men shake hands and then shake their heads as if to say, 'What were we all worried about?' My mother and I hug, and Bonnie joins in and then we ask if we can all go and see her.

'In a little while,' the doctor tells us. But he says Robert can go in straight away.

'Are you sure you don't mind?' Robert asks me. I give him

222

a quick hug.

'Of course not. Give her my love, OK?'

Now we know she's out of danger, I tell the others they might as well go home once we've seen her. Robert and I will stay behind; I'll happily stay all night if she wants me to.

Billy pulls me to one side as we leave the family room. 'Stel,' he says, hunching his shoulders. 'I just wanna say, that, erm –'

'Hang on a minute, Billy,' I interrupt. 'There's something I'd like to say first.'

'Oh.'

He looks a bit put out. I get the feeling he's been rehearsing his words and I've just taken the wind out of his sails. I put my arm around his narrow shoulders. 'Listen, bruv. I just want to say that I'm sorry I gave you such a hard time when you went away. We all deal with stuff in our own way, don't we?' See, that wasn't so hard, was it? Actually, it *was* quite difficult. But worth it. My brother's face melts into a goofy smile and he throws his arms around me.

'I love you, sis,' he says in a breaking voice.

'Well, OK then.' I pat his back awkwardly. I guess it's been an emotional night.

'I've got a job,' he tells me. I raise my eyebrows.

'Is that so?'

'That's why I couldn't make it to your decorating party. Didn't Mum tell you?'

I shake my head, ashamed of myself for thinking the worst of him yet again.

'It's only labouring, but it means I've been able to give Mum something to help her out. And I'm saving up, Stella. To pay you back the money I borrowed.' He gives me that goofy smile again and I feel something inside of me tear just a little.

'Thanks, bruv,' I say. Now it's my turn to sound choked.

He gives me a searching look. 'I'm sorry Paul didn't make it. You've still not talked?' I shake my head, not trusting myself to speak. Billy sighs. 'I know that he really cares for

223

you, Stel.'

'He's got a funny way of showing it.' We smile at each other and then go in for another hug, laughing for reasons neither of us could explain.

My mother is watching from the doorway and the look on her face is one of hopeful joy. I jerk my head to tell her to come over and quick as a flash she's right there in the circle of hugs. Now Bonnie joins in and we're all laughing at how funny we must look.

Robert comes out of Lipsy's room and says, 'Have I missed something?'

We pull him into the melee; the poor bloke probably didn't think the night could get much worse.

'How is she?' I mouth over Bonnie's head. Robert nods gravely.

As we break up and move towards the door I have a strange sensation. While Robert leads the way, and Billy guides my mother and Bonnie by the elbows, I reach out to the side to hold someone's hand. But there is no one there. I knew that already, of course. I just acted automatically, expecting a hand to be there to take mine. Immediately I realise my mistake, dropping my hand and giving my brother a little shove in the back. Thank God nobody saw me. I think I might be losing my mind.

**

Paul

Paul pushed through the double doors, dread making his stomach feel like it was full of stones. He hated hospitals, hated the smell and the fake-cheerful colours on the walls, and the ever-present air of disaster waiting to happen. He even hated the way the skirting boards were moulded into the walls; a cleaning aid, obviously, but it just seemed so institutional.

Scanning the waiting room, his eyes lighted upon Billy, leaning against the far wall with his familiar slouch. Paul hurried over, feeling slightly less anxious; Billy's body language wasn't giving off a sense of impending doom.

He was relieved to be right. 'She's going to be fine,' Billy told him. 'They've got the baby on a heart rate monitor to be certain, but it's looking good.'

'Thank God.' Paul slumped into a nearby chair and, after a brief pause, Billy joined him.

'What took you so long to get here, mate?'

Paul looked up in surprise and then turned away guiltily when he saw the look on Billy's face. 'I was out on a viewing,' he lied.

'Really? Stella said she was sitting outside your place when she got the call and that your car was there. Weird.' Billy gave a little shrug.

Paul was about to launch into an explanation but then he thought better of it. Billy wasn't the type to quiz him; he was far too laid back. Besides, he didn't have an explanation – he'd been ignoring his phone. God, did he feel bad about that now. One missed call from Billy, at least seven from Stella. And all the while he'd been watching TV, feeling sorry for himself.

'I wish I'd got here sooner,' Paul said to break the silence. 'Poor Lipsy. She must have been really scared.'

'We all were. Robert, Mum, Stella, Bonnie.'

Paul got the message loud and clear: everyone else had been here, everyone except him.

'As I said, I was on a viewing and I didn't –'

'Yeah, whatever.' Billy got to his feet with a sigh, shaking his hair out of his eyes. 'I'm going to go and see how they're doing. You might as well go home, mate.'

Paul stood as well and followed Billy's eyes down the long, green corridor. 'Is Stella still here? Do you think I could see her? Just so she knows I came.'

'I'll tell her, don't worry about it.'

'Well, I'd really like to see her. Make sure she's OK.'

Billy's expression was weary as he held up his hand and said, 'She's fine. I'll explain about the viewing. And I'll tell her you came. But I don't think it's a good idea for you to hang around, to be honest. It's been an emotional day, Stella doesn't need any more upset.'

'But I'm not going to upset her,' Paul protested.

'You already have, mate.'

Paul watched in astonishment as Billy walked slowly away. He never thought he'd be on the receiving end of a telling-off from Stella's brother, of all people. Suddenly being all protective. As if Stella needed protecting from him.

'Hey, Billy! Wait up!' Paul raced down the corridor after Billy's retreating back.

A passing nurse glared at him sternly. Paul mumbled sorry and slowed his pace. He reached Billy just before the doors and grabbed his arm. 'Wait a second, will you?'

Billy turned around and regarded Paul with an unreadable expression.

'Look, I'm sorry I didn't pick up the phone. It was stupid of me. I was sulking and now I feel terrible. I know I should have spoken to Stella, given her a chance to explain, I just … Oh, I don't know. What with Lipsy's dad being around all the time and then seeing her coming out of her neighbour's like that, I just–'

'Thought the worst?' Billy finished for him. Paul nodded sheepishly.

'I should have trusted her. I know she's not a liar. But I guess I was scared.'

'Of what?' Billy seemed genuinely bemused.

'Of messing it up again.' Paul sighed and leaned against the wall, watching a group of student doctors rush past, white coats flying out behind them like wings. 'Did she tell you about that day when she kind of came on to me?' Billy shook his head. 'Well, I blew it big time then. I hadn't realised, you see. Hadn't really admitted to myself how I felt about her. I thought I wanted the whole bachelor thing. It took a lot to make me open my eyes.'

Billy was watching him carefully. 'And now?' he said. 'Are you sure about what you want now?'

Paul nodded. 'Although it looks like I've left it too late. If she's gone back with John Dean I guess it serves me right.'

'She hasn't gone back with that loser. My sis has got more sense than that. For your information, she met up with him to tell him where to go. And, true to form, he did go. To Bristol, by the sounds of it. Didn't even say goodbye to his own daughter. So it looks like you got that one wrong, doesn't it?' Billy shook his head and stretched out his spine. 'God, this new job is killing me.'

Paul was still digesting this new information. So what Loretta had seen was Stella breaking up with John Dean, not her getting together with him. How could she have got it so wrong? How could *he* have listened to Loretta instead of just going and asking Stella what was going on? But then, he had gone, hadn't he? And look what he'd found…

'So, her neighbour?' Paul asked. He was starting to feel very foolish. 'I expect I got that wrong too, did I?'

'You betcha!' Billy said cheerfully. 'Spilled a load of red wine over herself and the one-man cleaning machine whipped off her clothes quick as you like. And put them straight in the wash.' He laughed loudly and nudged Paul in the ribs. 'The geezer must be gay, don't you think? I mean, it's a perfect ploy for getting a girl naked but he never laid so much as a finger on her.'

Shaking his head as if this was the funniest thing he'd ever heard, Billy pushed through the double doors and was gone.

Chapter 26

Lipsy

Saturday 4*th* August

I've had to pretend that I'm tired just to get them all out of my room. They haven't left me alone since Thursday night and I feel like I'm suffocating. Rob has set up his sleeping bag beside my bed here – I told him he could get in with me if he liked but he said it didn't seem right under my mum's roof. Who'd have thought he'd have turned out that way? And they all thought he was the bad influence on me!

Mum said Rob can move in with us which is so nice of her. The truth is we can't afford our own place at the moment, there's just no way. But Mum has this plan to buy another house and do it up, and she said that if we help her then we could live there, rent-free. I said she'd never make it as a property developer if she did that but she just looked at me and smiled. Anyway, Rob and I have talked about it and we're going to do more than just help her – we're going to do practically all of the work and then we're going to pay her a proper rent. It's the least she deserves.

The baby inside me is doing fine. It's nine and a half weeks now, the size of either a lemon or an olive, depending on which book you believe. I had a "close call" apparently and now I have to spend the rest of my pregnancy taking it very easy. I don't mind, though. The thought of losing my baby makes me feel sick. I have this picture in my head of it inside me, all helpless and funny-shaped, and it's saying 'Don't worry, Mummy, I'm OK.' When I think this I want to cry, but I feel happy at the same time. Weird, huh?

There is just one thing I regret, and boy is my mum going to be smug when I tell her. I regret that I didn't do better at school. After the baby's born I want to be one of those working mums with a suit and scraped-back hair and everyone else going on about how well they cope. So I guess I need to go to college – maybe this September if the doctor lets me, or next year if not. Next year's OK, I suppose. I haven't told anyone about my plans yet, not even Rob. I hope he understands. He's so protective. I love him to bits, I really do. But he's got to realise that I'm too young to just stay at home and bring up his kid. I need to have a life too, one that includes a baby and a bloke but is kind of mine at the same time.

I think my mum will understand. My mum seems to understand everything these days. Except how to sort out her own life, of course. After that awful night when Paul caught her coming out of Joshua's she's not really been herself. She says she's still annoyed at him cause he didn't turn up at the hospital for me, but I did point out to her that he made it there in the end, so it wasn't as if he didn't care.

Not like my own dad. But I'm not surprised. Some people just aren't cut out to be part of a family. I guess I'm lucky.

* * *

Stella

This Sunday is the first in ages where I haven't had to don a hideous yellow shirt and serve coffee with a smile at Café Crème. With my career as a waitress behind me, and my job at Smart Homes seriously in question, I've come to see my mother to find out what she thinks about me and Dad going into business together.

I'm surprised how positive she is about the whole thing.

I'd have thought she'd be a bit wary, not want him to get involved in anything that might take him away from her. But she's all for it, even suggests using the family name for the business.

'"Hill Homes" always had a bit of a ring to it, don't you think?' She's clearing out her kitchen cupboards and I'm helping. That is, I'm sitting drinking tea while she cleans them. Moral support I call it.

'You don't think it's a little – tainted?' I ask, thinking that the company name would probably stay on the Inland Revenue's hit list for some time to come.

'I suppose it might be.' She is smiling and I realise that she was winding me up. My mother doesn't have a sense of humour, as far as I know, so this takes me by surprise.

'I suppose we could call it "Inside Job",' I say, wondering if she'll get the joke.

She does. Well, wonders never cease. I go to kneel next to her and start to wipe the pans and pot lids she's piling up at her side. 'So you don't think it will be too much for him?' I ask her, wiping two years' of dust from a casserole dish.

My mother shakes her head. 'I think it will be just what he needs. A project, something to get his teeth into.'

'Yeah, that's what I thought too. You could get involved, if you like,' I say generously. I haven't really thought this through, but it makes sense in a way. I'm not sure what she'd do, exactly. Not shopping for finishing touches, that's for sure, not with her eye for tat.

'That's a nice thought, Stella. Thank you. But I couldn't, I'm afraid.'

'Oh. Why?'

'I have a job. Starting next month.'

'A job?'

'At the school. It's only part-time but it's something.' She looks down at the baking tray in her hand. 'I want to contribute, to take the pressure off your dad when he comes home.'

231

'That's great, Mum, well done. You're not going to be a dinner lady are you?'

'As a matter of fact I am.' Oops. 'We're called Lunchtime Assistants now, though.'

'That's great, Mum,' I say again, giving her a little hug and a pat on the back. 'Don't let those little horrors give you any grief.'

'I won't,' she says seriously. 'I've had quite enough grief, thank you.'

In the past, I would have taken this as a dig at me – probably with good reason. But this time I let it pass with a chuckle and she laughs too, and then I'm aware that we are having a nice time, my mum and me, just hanging out, doing stuff. I want to tell her, 'See, you don't have to go shopping to have a good time,' but I don't.

Instead, I have one of those spooky flashbacks where I remember Lipsy saying almost exactly the same thing to me recently. And I realise that this was what bothered me at the time: she was accusing me of being the same as my mother.

I sit back on my heels to think about it. Do I really use shopping as a substitute for having a life? Do I look for "stuff" to make me happy, to give my life meaning, the way my mum does? I'd like to say a categorical 'No' but then I remember my list of things I can't live without and how heavy it is with rather pointless objects.

'Penny for them,' my mother says to me.

'They're not worth a penny,' I tell her, truthfully.

I go back to cleaning, trying to shake off this feeling that is threatening to spoil my good mood. My mother has another bit of news for me: she has a new lodger.

'At least Billy's here now to keep an eye on you,' I say, rolling my eyes.

'Oh, don't be such an old woman, Stella.'

Well, excuse me for caring!

'Besides,' she says. 'It's a girl. Anne's daughter – remember Anne? – is working at the hospital and she needs a place to stay. Her mum and dad are paying her rent so it's pretty much guaranteed. Isn't that great?'

I nod, unsure. 'But what about when dad gets home? Don't you want to have the place to yourselves?'

She shifts herself over to the next cupboard and I follow, shuffling on my knees. 'Ideally,' she says. 'But we don't live in an ideal world, Stella. Sometimes you have to make sacrifices, have things not quite as you want them so you can have them right one day. I've made a lot of mistakes – and other people have paid for them. Mainly your father.' I look away at this. We still haven't really discussed it and I'm not sure I want to. It's between the two of them, nothing to do with me. If my dad forgives her then that's all that matters.

As if reading my mind, she says, 'If you're very, very lucky sometimes you get a second chance. And if you're very, very clever, you don't blow it.' She smiles at me and I wonder if she's always been this wise or if it's a recent acquisition.

'Sometimes,' she carries on, rubbing an ugly old teapot absently, 'you have to back down, be the one to say you're sorry. If you don't want to lose the person you love.'

It seems as though she's still talking about herself and dad here, but I'm starting to see through it. I'm not stupid. She is talking about me and Paul.

'And sometimes it's only by doing the backing down that you can show someone how much you love them. Don't you think?' she turns to look at me, her face an open book.

But not one I'm about to read.

'Is that the time?' I look at my wrist even though I don't wear a watch. 'I've got to go.' And I'm out of the door before she can try and stop me.

Honestly, some people. They just don't know how to quit when they're ahead.

233

Chapter 27

Stella

First thing Monday morning I hand in my notice at Smart Homes.

This has not been a snap decision. I spent all last night thinking about it. And this morning, as I crept around the house so as not to wake Lipsy, I asked myself, 'What have you got to lose?'

The answer? A regular salary and possibly a best friend but apart from that, nothing. And sometimes – this is my own brand of wisdom, not my mother's – sometimes you have to let something go to make room for something better. Create a vacuum. Nature hates a vacuum, apparently.

Of course, I don't mean Paul. I'm not planning on making room for someone better than him – I don't think such a person exists. Except for his fatal flaw of always believing the worst about me and being too stubborn to talk about it, he's my ideal man.

And I've gone and ruined it. Of course I'm upset, but maybe not as upset as I would be if I was ten years younger. At my age, you learn to take things in your stride. Besides, I never really had him did I? Can't miss what you never had.

Oh, who am I kidding? I'm devastated, and when I walk into the office and see him in his navy suit (my favourite), my legs turn to jelly and I need to sit down immediately. Maybe I should stay working here just so I can see him every day.

Maybe in time we'd get around to sorting it all out and build up our friendship all over again.

Or maybe I'd turn into a shrivelled old prune watching him get together with some gorgeous other woman, meanwhile abandoning my dreams and my father to boot.

I stand up tall and square my shoulders, marching into Paul's enclave as though it's the most natural thing in the world. 'Here,' I say, thrusting the envelope at him. The letter inside was hastily handwritten this morning. 'You probably won't be too disappointed to get this.'

He looks at me and then at the white envelope. 'What is it?' The sound of his voice makes me want to cry. I notice that his eyes are red and he looks like he hasn't slept in days either.

'It's my notice,' I tell him, trying to keep my voice steady. 'I've given you a month but I'm thinking you most likely just want to see the back of me.' Giving him my bravest smile I say, 'So I can pack up and leave now if you want me to.'

Inside I'm thinking: Please don't let me go, please tell me to stay.

He looks like he's just been smacked in the mouth. For a second the room seems to spin, the ground underneath me unsteady. I wonder if I am making a huge mistake. Then something passes over his face and his expression becomes unreadable. 'If that's what you want,' he says quietly. 'Go now if you want to. I guess we can manage.'

'OK,' I say, wishing I didn't sound as though I was about to cry. 'I will then.'

And I turn on my heel and walk back into the office, where the stunned silence tells me that everyone has heard every word. The sooner I get out of here the better.

At my desk, I quickly pack a box with my pathetic personal effects: a fluffy pen Lipsy bought for me; a birthday card from Bonnie with a particularly hunky bloke on it; a toy bear wearing a knitted jumper, a present from Paul. This I decide to leave behind.

Loretta snakes across the room and perches by her desk.

'You're not *leaving* us are you, Stella?' she says in her sugary-sweet voice.

I stand up and slowly walk over to her. I know this mess was partly her doing, and I know what she hopes to gain by it. I also know she has absolutely no chance with Paul, and I'm almost sorry I won't be around to watch her crash and burn.

With one good slap I could wipe that self-satisfied smile off her face and give her something to remember me by. Maybe it would make her think twice before messing with anyone else. I lean in. She shrinks back. It's so tempting. What do I have to lose? Not my job. And not Paul.

Only my self-respect.

Standing in the middle of the office, I look around and take in the glossy displays, the banks of filing cabinets and the familiar furniture. I take a deep breath and smile at Susan and Joe, and then I look back at Loretta.

'You know what?' I tell her, still smiling. 'You're not worth it, Loretta. You're a sad little woman with no life, and I'm moving on to bigger and better things.'

There is a little squeal behind me and Susan starts clapping. Joe joins in, before breaking off and looking down, embarrassed. I give Susan a wide grin and tell her, 'Don't let her start on you now, OK?'

'Don't worry,' Joe buts in, fixing Loretta with a steely look. 'I won't let that happen.'

Now it's Susan's turn to look embarrassed. Well, well. Seems there's been more than one romance blossoming at Smart Homes. I hope this one's more successful.

I look across to Paul's cubbyhole, but all I can see is the back of his head. This would be a good time for him to come out and wish me luck for the future. Better still, come out and tell me he's sorry, and he loves me and wants to be with me forever.

But he doesn't come out at all.

So I walk out into the Milton Keynes' sunshine and leave

Smart Homes behind me without a second glance.

I am moving on to pastures new. I am completely terrified.

Chapter 28

Stella

Paul plays heavily on my mind, particularly when I'm asleep. I have these vivid dreams, every one of them featuring a blissfully happy Paul and me indulging in some bizarre or outrageous activity, like mud-wrestling in chocolate or flying over a mountain astride a silky black horse. Bonnie says it is my subconscious mind putting me in touch with my secret desires while simultaneously exorcising my failure to secure the love of my life. But then Bonnie says a lot of things. Especially when she's drunk.

I am trying to get to sleep in her spare room after an excruciating dinner party where I've been introduced to not one but two "eligible" single blokes that Bonnie and Marcus think would be perfect for me. They weren't.

To be honest, I only agreed to go through with the charade because I am sick to death of being alone in my house with no TV and no Lipsy. I even miss Robert. The two of them – the three of them – have gone away for a fortnight to Robert's parents' caravan in Southend. Classy, I said. Don't be such a horrible snob, Lipsy said. We argued about it; some things never change.

But things are fine between us now, all that tiptoeing around replaced by something more robust. I can tell her that her room is a mess or her music's too loud, and she can tell me to sod off and mind my own business. And a few minutes later we're laughing and it's all forgotten. I never had that relationship with my own mum. I like it a lot.

At this precise moment in time, my granddaughter-to-be is ten whole weeks old inside the womb. I'm not so dense that I don't realise this means the baby was almost certainly conceived the weekend of the fire. How strange that these two events should have started in motion the worst run of luck I've ever had.

Maybe I just had to go through the crap stuff to get to the good stuff.

I wish that included Paul, though. I really do. As I sat at Bonnie's dining table tonight, eating something Marcus had concocted from the latest Jamie Oliver book (that man has a lot to answer for), I felt as though a part of me was missing. I should be part of a couple, with Paul at my side, laughing and joking with each other in that exclusive way couples have, rolling our eyes at the other's exploits, sneaking off into the kitchen for a cuddle under the pretence of getting more wine.

There was no chance of Bonnie pairing me off tonight. Or any other night. Mr Smart is a hard act to follow, and he fills my head like the chicken and potato flan fills my stomach now. Except by the morning the meal will be gone, magically absorbed by my greedy body, but Paul will still be inside my head. There is no cure for love. Not when you've lost it.

Bonnie comes in with a coffee and some toast. I'm confused. 'Is it morning already?' I ask. I do feel quite groggy.

'No, stupid.' She sets them down on the bedside table and perches herself on the edge of the bed. 'I thought it would help to sober you up.'

'And stop me sleeping. All that caffeine.'

'Whatever.' My friend wriggles her backside further onto the bed. 'Move your great big legs,' she says. Thanks, Bonnie. So good for my self-esteem.

'I've been thinking,' I tell her.

'Oh, no.' She rolls her eyes to the ceiling.

'No, wait. I've been thinking about Paul.'

'Yes, that's what I thought you were going to say. Don't do it to yourself, Stella. You've had more ups and downs with that man than I've had in the lift. And I've lived here for five years. That's a lot of trips in a lift.'

I nod but carry on regardless. 'We have been through a lot together, Paul and I. He's been a good friend to me, that counts for a lot. I don't know, Bon. I was upset with him for jumping to the wrong conclusions and then ignoring me but he has been trying to get in touch. Or at least he was up until a few days ago.'

The missed calls on my mobile, which had made me feel so justified and in control while I was still hurt and angry, have now dried up completely. It's hard to read anything into this other than that he's simply given up. It's like it turned into a competition in the end – who could be the most stubborn. It looks like I won. Talk about winning the battle and losing the war!

'It just seems wrong to give up without one last try,' I say sadly, drawing my knees up to my chest. Bonnie makes the most of the space on the bed, flopping back with a groan.

'Now, don't be taking this the wrong way,' – which, of course, I'm bound to now she's said that – 'but here you are, a thirty-eight-year-old woman –'

'Thirty-seven!'

'Thirty-seven, then. And you're sleeping in your best friend's spare room because you have no TV and you hate being on your own.' She purses her lips together and tilts her head. 'Don't you think that's just a little bit sad?'

You won't be my best friend much longer if you keep making comments like that, I want to say.

But don't. Because she has a point.

'If that's true,' I say instead, 'then this might be my last best chance to do something about it. In fact,' I throw the covers back and swing my legs out of the bed, 'that's exactly what I'm going to do! I'm going to go and see Paul and I'm going to bloody well make him listen to me. If there's any

241

chance at all of us getting together then I'll find out – and I won't take no for an answer.'

Bonnie watches me pick up my bag and stuff my toothbrush and shoes inside it before she says, 'Don't you think it might be better to wait until morning? Like, he might take you a bit more seriously if you were dressed in something other than pyjamas?'

'Right,' I say and flop back down on the bed. 'The morning it is then.'

Only one problem. I seem to have spent so long avoiding him, I have absolutely no idea what I'm going to say.

* * *

'Where are you off to?' Bonnie emerges from the bathroom the next morning looking like the bride of Dracula and rubs her eyes to make sure that the apparition of me in full jogging regalia is not a figment of her imagination.

'Jogging,' I reply.

'Stella,' she groans, reaching blindly for the kettle. 'You do not jog.'

'I do now,' I say gaily, jogging on the spot to prove a point. 'Where's Marcus?'

'He has a meeting today.' Bonnie puts tea bags and milk in two cups. 'Toast?'

'Defo!'

She gives me a weary look. I stop jogging.

'Working on a Saturday, eh? He's keen.'

'We're saving.' She grabs the butter from her enormous fridge – a carbon copy of my beloved double-door ice-maker. How I mourned that fridge. Now I just think how stupid it must have looked in my cute little kitchen.

'You're both loaded. What could you be saving for?'

'Stella,' Bonnie says, turning to face me, marmalade jar in hand. 'I've been meaning to tell you this but kind of waiting for the right time, with all your troubles and stuff.'

'What?'

She looks uncomfortable. 'The thing is, Marcus has asked me... he and I are getting married.'

Just then the toast pops up and we both look at it, shocked. I break the silence first. 'That's fantastic, Bonnie! I'm happy for you. You make a lovely couple.'

And I mean it, I really do. It is hard, hearing that your best friend's getting hitched when you're – what was it Bonnie called me last night – "a bit sad". But I am genuinely happy for her.

Everything's changing, it seems. Everyone's moving on.

I eat my toast while she tells me about their plans: spring wedding, new house, babies soon after hopefully.

Hugging her, I tell her I've got to go.

'Where are you off to?' she asks.

'I told you, I'm going jogging.'

'Seriously?'

'Seriously.'

'But...' She looks me up and down. 'Where did you get the gear from?'

'Home.'

'You went home to get changed and then came back here again?' Bonnie looks puzzled. 'Not that it isn't lovely seeing your ugly mug over breakfast but why?'

I shove the last of the toast into my mouth and swallow. 'Because,' I tell her, resuming my jogging on the spot, 'I have no food in the house. And what I'm about to do requires a full stomach. Wish me luck!' With that, I give her a quick hug and jog right out of the door.

You may have guessed that there is an ulterior motive to my new-found exercise plan. In fact, it is more of a one-off than a plan. As I drifted into a fitful sleep last night I remembered that the object of my love and affection is very much a creature of habit and that his habits are wholesome and healthy. They involve games of squash, healthy eating – and running around Willen Lake every morning without fail.

Chapter 29

Stella

Perversely, despite being the middle of August and the height of the British summer, this morning it is surprisingly cold. I've already been around the blasted lake twice and still haven't warmed up. Admittedly I've been walking rather slowly instead of jogging, but I don't want to meet Paul looking like Sweaty Betty for this, my last chance at happiness.

Eventually, I see him. He emerges from the trees looking like an advert for Adidas, running at the pace of an athlete. My heart misses a couple of beats, despite the lack of exertion. Gamely, I begin jogging, and before long can hear his footsteps behind me. As he passes I step into his path, timing it perfectly. Although I hadn't meant for him to fall headlong into the bushes.

Oops.

'Are you OK?' I reach for his hand, surreptitiously smoothing my hair out of my face at the same time.

Paul stands and brushes himself down, then stares at me as though I'm from another planet.

'What the hell are you doing here?' he says.

Not a friendly planet, obviously.

'Jogging,' I say brightly, trying to make out I am as surprised as him. 'Fancy seeing you here!' But he is clearly having none of it.

'Are you stalking me?' he asks suspiciously.

The very idea! 'No, I am not.' I make my face indignant. 'I'll have you know I'm merely keeping fit. Lots of people run around the lake, as you see.' I wave my arm in a wide arc but unfortunately, we seem to be the only two people in Milton Keynes at that moment. I've never seen Willen Lake less crowded.

'OK. Well, I'll let you get back to it then.' Paul starts to jog away.

No! This isn't the way it is supposed to happen.

'Paul, wait!' I call.

He carries on running. I have no choice. I must subjugate myself and run after him.

Huffing and puffing, I chase along the gravel path, too out of breath to call out again, while all the time he runs faster and faster. He obviously knows I'm behind him. He has no intention of making it easy for me. So he's still playing the game of stubborn, is he? At this rate I will be dead by the time I catch him up, never mind sweaty.

Suddenly he stops, and this time it is me who runs headlong into him. He thrusts out his hand and grabs me, waiting until I've found my feet before he drops my arm. He regards me thoughtfully. I try to speak, can't, so I hold up my palm while I catch my breath. All the while those piercing blue eyes are on me like a judgement.

'Paul,' I say finally, trying to ignore the sweat that is dripping off the end of my chin.

Come on, Stella. Don't blow it now.

'The thing is,' I begin again, 'I was kind of hoping to bump into you today.' His expression says, No shit? I press on. 'I wanted to talk you. I wanted to say that I'm sorry for ignoring your calls. I was...' Trailing off, I wonder how to explain the complicated feeling of anger and indignation mixed with desire and fear that had stopped me every time I went to pick up the phone.

'It's OK,' he says calmly. 'I understand.'

'You do?' I struggle to get past his closed expression, desperate to know what is going on in his head right now. 'Well, anyway, we could talk now if you like. If there's something you've been wanting to tell me, some reason for the phone calls...'

I've given him an in. All he has to do now is step up and take it. I can't take my eyes off the gravel path. My heart is beating furiously and it has nothing to do with the running.

After a long silence, Paul says, 'It doesn't matter now.'

I look up at him in shock. 'What do you mean, it doesn't matter? Of course it matters. You must have phoned me about fifty times.'

'And you must have ignored me about fifty times,' he snaps back quickly.

We seem to have reached another impasse. The sweat is starting to dry on my skin, making me cold and shivery. Don't leave it like this, the sensible voice in my head is saying. Try one more time.

I cross my arms over my chest, then uncross them again immediately. No defensive body language. Instead, I step forward slightly so I'm close enough to see the shadow of his eyelashes on his cheeks. This is going to be really, really hard. But not doing it would be harder.

'I've never told you this before, Paul, although I'm thinking that there is a part of you that must already know. I had a terrible crush on you at school. I was in love with you, really had it bad, as bad as it gets. But the truth is, even though I thought it had gone away when I grew up and we became friends, it never did. I love you. I've always loved you. And I think – I think you might feel the same way about me.'

God, that was hard. But it's out there now, no going back. I risk a glance upwards at his face again. If anything I've said has registered it doesn't show. His expression is as impassive as before. No wonder he's a good poker player.

Maybe he didn't hear me. Maybe he couldn't take it in after everything that's happened.

'What I'm saying, Paul, is that I'm in love with you, although I didn't know it for a long time, because obviously if I had I would have done something about it sooner. You were there all the time, right under my nose, but I didn't see it. I mean, you take it for granted, don't you, what's there in front of you? You don't realise what's really important until it's gone. Like all the stuff I lost in the fire. I thought all that was important for a while. I thought I'd never be happy again until I replaced every last thing ...

'But now I know I was wrong – all that stuff doesn't mean anything, it's totally worthless. You joked about how I'd probably save my fridge-freezer before my family photos, Paul, and maybe you were right – then. But I've learned a lot in these last few months. I've learned what really matters. And what matters is... what matters is...'

I take a deep breath. This is all getting away from me somehow. I need to get it back on track.

'Once I realised how I felt about you I tried to let you know. And it didn't go down too well, did it? I was embarrassed, it was hard to be rejected. But then I started to see that maybe you did feel something for me, and we started to get closer and it was great. But all the time it was like all you could see were the other people in my life, people like John Dean and Joshua – people who weren't important. You weren't seeing me. And you were punishing me for things I hadn't even done. It was unfair.'

I wish he'd say something back instead of letting me prattle on. But Paul seems to be made of stone. I honestly don't think he has moved a muscle since I started talking. I am shivering now and I just know that my nipples are sticking out ridiculously. Not that Paul is the kind of man to comment on a thing like that. Which is one of the reasons I love him so much.

'Paul.' I try hard to keep the note of pleading out of my voice. 'I'm sorry it all got messed up, I really am. Yes, I was a bit confused about John Dean at first. And yes, I am friends with Joshua, but that's all it will ever be. I know my priorities were all over the place for a while. And we've both been too stubborn to sort it out. But I know now that the one thing in my life that I can't live without is you.'

In my whole life I have never said anything so clichéd. But I have an idea that when something is true it ceases to be a cliché. I watch his beautiful face and I wait, feeling as though time has stopped.

Here, by the side of the lake, with the goose poo giving off nose-curling fumes at our feet, I wait. But Paul just stands there looking over my head across the water, like a marble statue with a face carved out of granite. The early morning sun highlights his cheekbones and makes his blue eyes shaded and unreadable. Time stretches out.

A woman with a dog walks past, moving onto the grass to give us a wide berth.

This is useless.

I turn and start back towards the car park, trying to run but mainly just stumbling. My legs are made of wood. And I never noticed before how tears sting your eyes – are they made out of acid or something? Just to punish you that little bit more.

When I reach my car I search inside my holdall for a tissue, cursing the fact that I still haven't learned to be more organised.

A small sheet of paper falls out onto my lap. I pick it up and unfold it carefully, peering out of teary eyes. It's that blasted list again, coming back to haunt me. All the things I thought I couldn't live without. An American double-door ice-maker fridge-freezer. A Kenwood mixer that I never even used. What a joke! None of it means anything anymore. I crumple the list into a sad little ball, throw it out of the window and drive away.

Chapter 30

Stella

Ten weeks and one day. That's how long it has been since I woke to find my house going up in smoke. And now, as I sit on my brand new sofa waiting for my brand new TV to arrive, just about everything is back to normal. Except, of course, nothing in my life is normal anymore.

But at least I have a working kitchen and a sparkling bathroom, and walls that smell of fresh paint instead of smoke. Everything in my life is brand new – just what I'd always wanted. A sparkling, untarnished version of what I had before.

On the surface at least.

This house is now a vastly improved version of its former self. Putting together everything I've learned from those wonderful TV programmes I have decorated in neutral shades, kept the clutter to a minimum, and gone for the best kitchen I could afford.

The sale of this house will fund my new career but I'm not in a huge rush to put it on the market. I've only just got it back – I want to enjoy it myself a little first.

I am wiping down my new granite-effect worktops for the tenth time this morning when there is a knock on the door. It's the telly men, panting under the weight of the plasma screen I've waited so long for. Even though it's only a measly thirty-seven inches (size isn't everything, you know), the delivery men make a right meal of bringing it in and getting the thing set up. By the time they've gone, I'm itching to see those tubes in action. Remote in hand, I sink back into the sofa. With a low hum and a hiss of static it springs to life and fills my lounge with colour.

The people on the screen are screeching at each other in mock-cockney accents. Everybody looks miserable. It's raining. Hmm. Sunday afternoon soap omnibuses haven't changed much since I've been away from the box. I press my shiny new remote control and another picture appears on the screen in glorious Technicolor. Lots of green, so bright I want to shield my eyes. And little figures of men running around then diving on the floor in agony.

Did I really spend all this time saving all this money just so I could watch EastEnders or football?

Finally, I settle for an episode of Columbo, which is so old and grainy it doesn't do my new TV any justice at all. I might as well be watching it on a fifteen-inch portable with a set-top aerial. Crisps and chocolate offer some comfort, and soon I'm curled up with a contentedly fat belly, surveying my suave new lounge with a property developer's eye. Not bad, I think. Not bad for ten weeks' work on a budget, with two jobs and a pregnant daughter.

I'm considering driving to the nearest off-licence to buy myself some champagne when there is another knock on the door. Figuring it's probably one of the neighbours come to check out the finished product, I race to open it. I'm in the mood for company.

I open my shiny new front door and come face to face with Paul Smart.

Last seen turned into stone by the side of Willen Lake.

'Paul!' I say, doing a great job of stating the obvious.

'Stella.'

This is all he says in reply, and it sounds a little short so maybe the statue thing hasn't worn off completely.

Inviting him in, I witter on about the new décor and the

carpet shade I'd finally chosen.

Why am I so bloody nervous?

I wish I wasn't wearing my old leggings with the saggy arse and a T-shirt of Lipsy's that reads "Come Get Me Big Boy". Mind you, considering that the last time he saw me I was dripping with sweat this is possibly an improvement.

That's when I notice he is smiling. The granite has been chiselled away to reveal an actual smile. A stunning, light-up-the-room kind of smile. And he is rummaging in his pocket for something. I resist the urge to offer to do that for him. Something tells me this is not the time for smut.

'What are you looking so happy about?' To be honest, I'm a bit annoyed. What right does he have to be smiling when I'm feeling so low. Yesterday I told the man I loved him. The last time I told a man that I was still a size ten.

Could he be any more insensitive?

'You know, Stella,' he says, still smiling, 'you really shouldn't be such a litterbug.'

So the man has come to my house, when we aren't even speaking as far as I know, to tell me not to drop litter?

'What are you talking about?' I snap.

'I found something of yours and I thought you might like it back.' Now his sexy smile is starting to get on my nerves. Paul is just too damn handsome when he smiles, and having to look at it now is like having my nose rubbed in the whole sorry mess all over again.

'Whatever it is,' I tell him, strolling through to the kitchen and talking over my very cold shoulder, 'I'm not interested. But thanks for stopping by.' I can't cope with another rejection. I don't have the strength. Better if I get the rejection in first this time: at least that way I'll have a shred of self-respect left.

'Here, have this.'

I look at his hands. They hold a crumpled piece of paper. Has he come round to give me a note? My P45, perhaps? I look again more closely. The colour of the paper looks familiar. It has balloons all over it and is a muddy shade of pink.

Paul is holding in his hand the list that I dropped in the park. I glare at it and then at him. Will I never be rid of the thing?

'No thank you,' I say, spitting each word out. 'I don't think I'll be needing it anymore.'

'Are you sure?' He smiles at me again and his eyes are laughing. 'It's just that there's something on this list that you don't have yet. Something I'd really like you to have. And you did put "Can't Live Without" at the top of the list, so I think you should take a look.' He holds it out at me, waving it tantalisingly in front of my face.

I snatch it from him, wishing he would just stop smirking. Obviously my list has been a source of great amusement to him, which doesn't surprise me at all. But I am not going to give him the satisfaction of hearing me explain it.

'Happy now?' I say. 'Well, if that's all I am a bit busy.' I wave at the kitchen with its sparkling surfaces and immaculately empty worktops. Clearly I have nothing at all to do.

Paul leans comfortably against the cooker and gestures at the plain white fridge-freezer. 'You decided not to replace the monster, then?'

I could quite happily throttle him. He looks so damn sexy in a suit. Come to think of it, why is he wearing a suit? On a Sunday? And why, after all I've said, is he still smiling at me?

'What about the last item on your list?' he asks again. 'Are you sure you've changed your mind about that one?'

'Will you just…' I am about to say something unrepeatable when I notice the look in his eyes. There is something indefinable there, a combination of excitement and affection. I haven't seen him look like that since he organised a surprise party for my twenty-fifth birthday – which was a disaster, but that's a different story.

He points to the scrap of paper in my hand again.

Oh, for goodness sake! Do I really need my nose rubbing in this? I am about to throw it in the bin when I notice that something has been added to the very bottom of the list in what looks like a bad forgery of my handwriting.

Two words.

Paul Smart.

Underlined twice.

And ticked.

I look up at him, bewildered, and see that he is beaming. I look down at the list again and then back at him. Does this mean what I think it means? Sometimes I can be a bit slow on the uptake and sometimes I can jump to the wrong conclusions. (I guess I'm in good company there.) I can hardly bear to allow myself to believe that this might mean what I so want it to mean. Maybe it's some kind of joke.

'Is this a joke? Does this mean…'

I don't get the chance to finish my sentence. Paul is pulling me into his arms – God, it feels so good – and murmuring something in my ear. I decide to allow myself to believe that this is happening. He's right here, holding me. I'm holding him tightly now and I'm not letting go for anything.

'Glad to see you've finally got your priorities right, Stella,' he says in a voice I've never heard before: husky and full of bad intentions. Then his lips meet mine and he kisses me with so much passion I can hardly breathe. He pulls away just long enough to say, 'By the way, just so you know, I love you too.'

We stand there, wrapped around each other, kissing and laughing and making promises and plans. But mostly kissing. Making up for lost time. There is a lot of time to be made up, about twenty years I reckon. And Paul seems as eager to get started as I am.

Just before I melt away completely, I fix him with a steely glare. 'You've still got to work your way up to the top of the list, you know.'

He pulls away just far enough to look deep into my eyes.

'You mean, try to be even more useful than a fridge-freezer that makes ice?'

Exactly.

'I think I can manage that.'

THE END

CAN'T LIVE WITHOUT

~~*American double-door ice-maker fridge-freezer*~~

~~*Kenwood food mixer*~~

~~*Cath Kidston Kitchenalia*~~

Furniture! (Sofa, dining table, chairs, beds,
*   wardrobes…)* ✓

Clothes: see sub-list ✓

TV - whatever ✓

~~*Lipsy - computer, Playstation, iPod, clothes…*~~

Carpets for entire house ✓

New bathroom suite and towels ✓

Tiling - bathroom and kitchen ✓

Bed linen x 4 - Marks & Spencer ✓

Paul Smart ✓

A message from Stella!

If you enjoyed my story you should head over to
www.joannephillips.co.uk and sign up to **Joanne's newsletter**. You'll be the first to hear about new books AND there's a whole page of Goodies for readers!

Read on for **bonus content** including the chance to write your own 'Can't Live Without' list and the first chapter in my next adventure: *The Family Trap*.

Author Note

Thank you so much for reading *Can't Live Without* - I hope you enjoyed the ups and downs of Stella's first story. I got the idea for this book when I was walking around Willen Lake one day (yes, it's a real place in Milton Keynes, England, and it's truly beautiful). I heard sirens in the distance and thought: What if you arrived home to find your house on fire? It got me thinking about the impact of losing 'material things', especially for someone who defined themselves around what they owned. Stella popped into my mind pretty much fully formed and the first draft of *Can't Live Without* followed. This revised and updated edition was released in 2021 with a gorgeous new cover to mark the launch of Book 3 in the series, *Growing Pains*.

Here is a list of my current books and you can find out more about me and my writing at www.joannephillips.co.uk or on social media. Please do get in touch, I love hearing from readers.

Happy reading!

Joanne

x

The Stella Hill Series of Romantic Comedies:
Can't Live Without
The Family Trap
Growing Pains
(more books in this series coming soon)

Romantic Comedies:
Cupid's Way
Hope Floats (coming soon)

Women's Literary Fiction:
Keeping Sam
This Beautiful World
You Are Here (coming soon)

Murder Mysteries:
Flora Lively and the Murder at the Maples
Flora Lively and a Date With Death
Flora Lively and the Sign of Seven

Non-fiction:
Get the Productivity Habit
Get the Mindfulness Habit
Get the Decluttering Habit

You don't have to lose everything to figure out what's important. Write your own list right here!

CAN'T LIVE WITHOUT

1.

2.

3.

4.

5.

6.

7.

8.

9.

10.

The Family Trap

Chapter 1

Get it out of me. Get. It. Out.'
My daughter is only seventeen, but today is possibly the best and the worst day of her life. Even though she's still my baby, right now she's trying to squeeze out her own baby into the waiting arms of a red-faced midwife.

Her gasps of pain bring back the memory of her birth with a force I hadn't expected and I want to reach for the gas and air in sympathy. They say you eventually forget the torture of giving birth – why else would any woman go on to have more than one child? We're brave, not masochists. Well, I only had one and I can tell you right now: a woman never forgets.

They also say nothing is more painful than giving birth. Wrong again. Watching your daughter in labour is far more painful. Right now I wish it were me lying there on the bed and not her.

What is it they also say? Be careful what you wish for. Sometimes I wish *they* would just shut up.

I'm standing away from the business end, holding my daughter's hand and mopping ineffectually at her forehead while she screams and swears at the midwife.

I push away the tiny part of me that is thinking: See?

You didn't listen did you, when I told you how awful it would be? You weren't careful, you didn't take precautions and now look at us. A slip of a girl, high on Pethidine, showing off an astonishingly varied vocabulary, attended by her single mum who still hasn't gotten used to the fact that any minute now she will become a grandmother.

A grandmother! At thirty-eight. There is so much wrong with this picture I don't know where to start.

Here comes Robert with fresh supplies of ice and chocolate, his face showing the strain of watching Lipsy suffer. Robert is one of those people who seem to be all one colour: his fine hair is the same pale biscuit shade as his skin; even his clothes are beige. He looks young for twenty-five but his hairline tells of problems to come.

That my daughter chose to fall in love with an older man tops off the craziness just perfectly, in my opinion.

'Stella?' says Robert, handing me the ice wrapped in a flannel. He's only recently stopped calling me Mrs Hill, even though I've never been a Mrs in my life. This is happily about to change in two weeks, but I won't be "Mrs Hill".

I take the flannel and apply it to the back of Lipsy's neck. She's on all fours now, panting like a marathon runner, her white T-shirt stuck to her back. Her long dark hair is matted at the crown like a fallen-out beehive, her lips vivid against fair skin.

I know why I'm dragging up stuff I thought I'd buried months ago. It's because I'm scared. No, terrified.

If I allow my mind to process what's happening in front of my eyes I'll be no use to my daughter at all. So I huff when she asks me for a glass of water, and I tut when Robert tenderly places a square of Bourneville in her swollen mouth.

'I need the toilet,' Lipsy croaks, her voice hoarse from shouting.

'Oh, for goodness sake,' is my response. It's how I'm dealing with it. Don't shoot me.

We shuffle her off the bed and move as one towards the toilet cubicle in the corner of the room – all of us, including Robert and the midwife, who has to drag the heart rate monitor and the drip stand across the floor. Somehow we manoeuvre this circus into the cubicle without anyone tripping up or pulling the line out of Lipsy's arm.

'Get lost then,' my daughter says. We stare at her, mouths open.

'I'm not doing a poo with you lot all watching,' she tells us defiantly. 'Aren't I allowed any privacy?'

I'm bizarrely proud of her for telling the woman who's been looking up her nether region for the last four hours to give her some privacy. It's ridiculous, it's completely pointless, and it's very, very Lipsy.

Robert is allowed to stay after some hissed negotiations ('You might fall over,' he points out, 'and you can't actually sit down or stand up again without help'), so the midwife and I shuffle backwards out of the toilet and take up our former positions.

'She's a feisty one,' she says. I notice her silver name badge reads *Maggie*. I smile to myself: Maggie is my mother's name. I take this as a good omen.

'Yes, she is. I think she takes after me.'

Maggie rolls her eyes. 'It's a shame she hasn't inherited your child-bearing hips though, eh?'

Suddenly I don't like this midwife very much at all.

***

Lipsy's baby is born in the toilet. Well, of course it is – nothing ever turns out the way it should in this family. Bearing down with all her strength, thinking herself mightily constipated, Lipsy finally managed what the midwife had been trying to achieve for hours. Thankfully Robert realised what was going on pretty quickly, and Maggie managed to dive in and ... well, I'll leave it there, shall I? There is such a thing as too much information. The first I heard about it was when Robert shouted, 'It's a boy', and ran out of the cubicle to hug me, before promptly collapsing at my feet.

'Hi, Mum.' Lipsy smiles at me weakly as I peer around the cubicle door. She's propped up against the far wall, surrounded by blankets.

'It's a boy,' she says, gazing down at the bundle in her arms, mesmerised. All I can see is one tiny pink fist, clenched as if in triumph. When Lipsy looks up at me again she is crying, the tears mingling with the sweat on her cheeks. Her face is swollen from all the fluids they've pumped into her and her skin is blotchy with broken veins. There's nothing beautiful about childbirth, that's for sure. But the sight of her hopeful expression breaks through my defences and I sink down by her side.

'I thought it was going to be a girl,' she says. 'I was going to call her Estelle.'

'Really?' Estelle is my name, although I've always preferred Stella. I tear my eyes from Lipsy's face to look for the first time at my not-to-be namesake.

And instantly I'm being dragged back through time – same hospital, same maternity ward, different midwife and very different circumstances, but this baby is surely the identical twin of the one I gave birth to seventeen years ago. Same big blue eyes, same spiky, matted black hair, same rosebud mouth with a slightly larger top lip. And the same soppy expression on my face, no doubt. Love and wonder, and complete devotion.

I hadn't expected this either. I hadn't expected to fall in love with Lipsy's baby the way mothers fall in love with their own. Maybe it's my hormones. Maybe it's the uncanny resemblance. Whatever it is, I just lost my heart to my grandchild. Despite everything I've said, I know I'll be a very proud lady the first time someone calls me Grandma.

'So what do you think, Grandma?' asks Lipsy.

Or maybe not.

OK, I'm not loving the Grandma label. But I guess I'll just have to get used to it.

'He's absolutely beautiful,' I tell her sincerely. 'And so are you,' I add, not quite so sincerely. She looks a complete fright, but the poor girl doesn't need to know that right now.

Lipsy hasn't always been so bothered about her appearance. But oh boy, once she started to grow a bump she became obsessed with her looks. I've tried telling her she'll get her figure back in no time, and that everyone's skin tone changes when they're pregnant, and that looks don't matter anyway – Robert loves her just the way she is – but generally she just glares at me like I'm offering up a future of unthinkable torture, then returns to her beauty magazines.

There'll be no beauty magazines now, I think, as I haul up off the floor to help the midwife move mother and baby back to the relative comfort of the hospital bed. It'll be all parenting magazines and Mumsnet and NCT groups. Unfortunately, I won't be there to suffer it along with her. In two weeks I'm changing my name to Mrs Paul Smart and moving to deepest darkest Derbyshire with the love of my life.

Which is really quite the worst timing I can think of. But, as Paul keeps reminding me, it's only a three-hour round trip, not the other side of the world.

Anyway, I've got other problems to dwell on right now. While Lipsy and Robert pose for the photo the midwife insists on taking (Lipsy will make me burn that later, I just know it), I finger the slim box in my pocket. Soon I'll head off to do my designated duty and let the rest of the family know that all is well. Paul will be waiting by the phone, and my mum and dad are probably on their way here already, unable to bear it any longer. And once I've worked my way down the list, then it will be time. I wanted to wait. Finding out beforehand didn't seem right, somehow.

'Mum,' calls Lipsy, 'come over here. We want to introduce you properly.'

I join them by the bed, where Robert is leaning over my daughter and looking very proud of himself. Not that he actually did anything... Well, maybe that's a bit unfair. But only a bit.

'Have you thought of a name?' I ask smiling. They've got dippy looks on their faces, the pair of them, and Lipsy looks fit to burst with excitement. The midwife is still in the toilet, hopefully clearing up the devastation.

'Yes,' Lipsy says with a grin. 'And you'll love it.'

'Well?' I look from Lipsy to Robert and back again. 'Tell me.'

'Mum, we'd like you to officially meet ... Phoenix.'

For about ten seconds I cannot speak. Here in the maternity suite, surrounded by bleeping instruments and bloody sheets, ten seconds feels like a lifetime. And then I hear a cough and a suppressed chortle coming from the toilet.

That woman has a nerve. First, she insults my hips, then she laughs at my grandson's name. Outrageous.

'Phoenix! How wonderful!' I exclaim, plastering a smile on my face and making my voice joyous. As I'm very, very tired I probably only manage happy, but that's enough for Lipsy.

'You like it? Oh, I'm so relieved. I thought you'd hate it. You know how you've always said symbolic names are really naff. But we thought it was cool because he was conceived on the night of the fire and the whole phoenix rising from the ashes thing?' She smiles up at

Robert, and then at me. 'Thanks, Mum. And thanks for being here for this. You were a star.'

Murmuring that it was nothing I look down at baby Phoenix. Oh, the poor child. Yes, I have often said that symbolic names are naff. Because they are! Rising from the ashes? Is the girl insane? A house fire caused by a faulty washing machine – a disaster compounded by zero house insurance – is hardly an event you'd want to commemorate by naming your child after it.

Phoenix turns his head slightly and appears to look directly into my eyes. I say appears to because it's a well-known fact that babies can't focus on anything so soon. Or maybe the scientists have it wrong. Because as baby Phoenix looks up at me, I'm absolutely certain I see the tiniest eye-roll. Oh great, he seems to say, and these pair are my parents? That's just wonderful.

***

It's nearly time for us to leave the maternity suite and head up to the ward. Visiting hours are relaxed for new fathers but not for new grandmothers, and I want to see Lipsy settled before I go home. But first, there is something important I must do. It's a task I've been putting off for weeks but it can't wait any longer.

I stroll nonchalantly over to the toilet cubicle, now mercifully spotless thanks to the hospital's crack cleaning detail and carefully lock the door. Then I take the slim box out of my pocket, pull out the white pen-shaped stick, and do the necessary. I don't need to read the instructions, I've already committed them to memory. Blue line means no baby, blue cross means shit hitting the fan at one hundred miles an hour. And so I wait, perched on the loo like a teenager waiting to have her future mapped out. The way my own teenager must have waited all those months ago.

If it comes to it, I just hope she's as understanding of my news as I was of hers.

As I watch, every cell in my body wishing for a blue line, the little window very clearly – and you could say proudly – starts to show a perfectly defined, bright blue cross.

There is a loud cry from outside the cubicle. Baby Phoenix is trying out his new and perfectly formed lungs. And inside here there is a helpless whimper. That's me. Today, the day I've become a grandmother for the first time and an expectant mum for the second time, is possibly the best and the worst day of my life.

Buy **The Family Trap** now to carry on reading!

Printed in Poland
by Amazon Fulfillment
Poland Sp. z o.o., Wrocław